The Forest Feast
MEDITERRANEAN

Simple Vegetarian Recipes
Inspired by My Travels

Erin Gleeson

Abrams
New York

Taormina, Sicily

Editor: Laura Dozier
Designer: Erin Gleeson
Production Manager: Denise LaCongo

Library of Congress Control Number: 2018958266

ISBN: 978-1-4197-3812-8
eISBN: 978-1-68335-651-6
B&N Edition: 978-1-4197-4440-2

ABRAMS The Art of Books
195 Broadway, New York, NY 10007
abramsbooks.com

For my favorite travel buddies:
Ezra, Jonathan & Max

Praia da Luz, Portugal

3

Castelbuono, Sicily
right: Cinque Terre, Italy

Riomaggiore, Italy

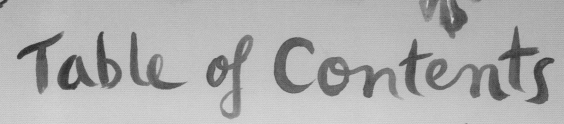

Table of Contents

Manarola, Italy

Bar Davi, Monterosso al Mare, Italy

Introduction

In the fall of 2017, my family and I set off for a journey through Spain, Italy, France, and Portugal. It's a privilege to be able to travel at all, but to be able to take three months off and go to Europe was a dream. My husband Jonathan had a sabbatical from work, and as an artist and author I am lucky to have a flexible schedule. Our kids are not in school yet, so we decided it would be the perfect time to do an extended trip.

We chose these destinations because I wanted to do recipe research for a Mediterranean-style cookbook I had been dreaming about. Even though the recipes in my previous books have a strong California influence, my style of cooking in general could be considered Mediterranean. Still, I was interested in learning more and tasting regional dishes in select parts of the Mediterranean firsthand—everything from tapas in Barcelona to pesto in Genoa.

During the trip, we visited countless restaurants and markets and I took endless notes and photos. And then after returning home, I set out to re-create my own vegetarian versions of the food we experienced on the trip, the best of which are featured in this book. While not necessarily authentic to each region we visited, the recipes in the pages that follow are inspired by the local dishes and ingredients we saw.

I was twenty-five when I met Jonathan, and after just a few months of dating, we took a big trip around Central America together. We found that we traveled well together and haven't really stopped since. But for this trip, with the luxury of time on our side, we realized that this adventure offered us a unique opportunity. We had the chance to really soak up a lifestyle far removed from our day-to-day and seek out inspiration for where our lives should go next. It's hard to believe it's been seven years since we moved from New York City to the woods of California, and in a way, we have missed city life. We miss walking everywhere, public transportation, and the rich culture that urban life offers. The cabin where we live, with its magical outdoor forest light, has been an amazing influence on my work and helped me produce three books, but I was ready for new inspiration.

I love to eat tapas-style, tasting many different flavors in a single meal, so Spain seemed like a natural place to start our trip, and the fact that Jonathan speaks Spanish was a bonus! I studied art for a year in Italy and also wanted to go back there (mostly for the gelato and pasta). I'd traveled a lot in Italy, but not much in Sicily, so we added it to the itinerary and I got to practice my rusty Italian. We couldn't pass up a stop on the stunning French Côte d'Azur en route to Italy, so we spent a week in Antibes. And for years we'd been wanting to visit Portugal, so we allotted about a month there. In three months, we visited four countries (five if you count a brief drive through Monaco), took six flights, rented four cars, took countless trains, and stayed in eleven different Airbnbs. Initially I was wary of moving around that much, but in the end, I wouldn't want to skip any part of it.

We learned a lot about traveling with kids on our trip. When we left, Max was nine months and Ezra was three years old. We packed all of our belongings into two rolling carry-on suitcases and two backpacks. As light as that sounds, we also needed to bring a travel highchair, two car seats, a travel crib, and a stroller. We had to be able to carry all of it and the baby from the plane to the taxi—and we could (barely).

Traveling with little kids who still need naps changes the course of your days as well. If we skipped naps, we paid for it, so we scheduled carefully around them. We did the bulk of our touring during the mornings and came back for "siesta" each afternoon. In many of the places we visited, businesses closed midday anyway, so we didn't feel like we were missing too much.

Because our kids go to bed before most restaurants open for dinner, we usually made lunches our "special" meals out. We arrived right when they opened for lunch, which meant fewer people to disturb and a better chance of getting a table outside where the kids could have a bit more space. Sometimes traveling with kids doesn't really feel like vacation, but little things like a glass of wine at lunch are relaxing and festive (and so European!). We are careful about screen time but did not hesitate to offer a show on the phone to our tantrum throwing toddler if we were at a nice restaurant or in a museum, which really helped as well. Overall, we found that our kids are quite adaptable, and to see each place through their curious eyes was an added pleasure. If you're debating taking a big trip with your kids, we say just do it!

There were so many amazing moments on our trip but when people ask us what our favorite stop was, we often say Barcelona. We began our adventure with an entire month in this city that we grew to love so much. If it were a bit closer to family, I think we could even see ourselves living there. We chose an apartment on the border of the Sant Antoni and Eixample neighborhoods, which was central but not touristy, and right near a metro stop. It was great to be in one place for an extended period of time at the beginning of the trip to get adjusted to the time change and to settle into life away from home. It was October, so we had the loveliest days and warm evenings. We set off each morning with our double stroller and got to know the city on foot. Evenings were mostly spent in our neighborhood, going to different plazas and sitting outside for tapas and a drink while Ezra played on the playground. Most playgrounds in Barcelona have an outdoor cafe directly in front of them, which I loved! (Why does that not exist in the States?)

Ordering vegetarian food when traveling can sometimes be frustrating. In Barcelona, I think we ordered patatas bravas, Spain's (much better) version of French fries, every night (see page 116). Our kids subsisted almost entirely on them and tortilla española (see page 156). But even with the inevitable repetition, I learned a lot. I enjoyed seeing eggs served in many different forms and not just for breakfast. Markets often offered interesting variations on traditional dishes, such as a vegetarian paella we saw in the Boqueria in Barcelona (see page 118). We also found some great vegetarian street food sold by small vendors, like the chickpea cake called socca in southern France (see page 160) and chickpea "fries" called panisette just across the border in Italy.

When I'm traveling, there's always the challenge of wanting to try the traditional, local dishes that happen to be vegetarian and simultaneously feeling like I'm missing out by skipping the famous meaty ones. And I often think I'm not getting the full, local experience if I go to the hip, new vegetarian restaurant, even though for some meals I might rather be eating that. So, for places we spent more time in, I opted to mix it up by sometimes eating at trendy, nontraditional places, but when visiting a city for only a couple days, I tried my best to experience the classic preparations, even if that meant eating some form of potatoes and eggs for every meal. I also kept a close eye on menus and asked servers about their local specialties to get ideas of what I could reimagine without meat back home.

We did splurge on a couple of fancy meals and I enjoyed the modern adaptations of traditional dishes using regional ingredients. Dinner in Spain happens quite late, so we got a babysitter a few times through an agency so that we could go out. The neighborhood in Barcelona we stayed in was in the middle of a culinary revival with many exciting restaurants and cocktail bars, including several Michelin-starred off-shoots by staff of the famous (but now-closed) restaurant El Bulli, such as one we tried called Hoja Santa. It is actually a Mexican restaurant, but I was interested in the idea of Spanish chefs using ingredients from Spain to create small dishes rooted in another place. The result was one of the more creative dining experiences I've had in terms of flavor and presentation. They served granita in a hollowed-out acorn squash, soup in an avocado shell, and a single piece of chocolate on a beautiful leaf. I aim to bring to my cooking these kind of thoughtful elements of color and presentation, so I came home with lots of new ideas.

We also took day trips outside the city. We took an hour-long train ride to the ancient, picturesque beach town of Sitges, where we swam in the sea and strolled the palm-lined promenade (see page 134). We took a cable car up a steep mountain to visit a monastery

and hiked to the top of Montserrat (see page 136). We wandered the cobblestone streets of Girona (see page 14) and rented a car to explore the beach towns along the Costa Brava, a stunning area I could have spent weeks in and hope to return to.

From Barcelona, we headed to the absolutely idyllic seaside town of Antibes, France, where we met Jonathan's parents for a week. We stayed in the old town, in a stone house that was actually part of the town's rampart, just steps from the lively outdoor farmers' market. We visited the market daily and they had the most beautiful offerings, even in November. We kept going back for the radishes, which we enjoyed with fresh French butter during cocktail hour at home (see page 21). Each evening in Antibes, we walked to a different restaurant in the old city for dinner. Highlights of our time in France also included day trips to the adorable towns of Èze and Saint-Paul-de-Vence (see pages 16 and 17).

One of my favorite stops was the Picasso Museum in Antibes, just a couple blocks from where we stayed. It's housed in a beautiful, old building on the sea that Picasso did an artist residency in years ago, and they have much of the art he created there on display. I loved imagining him working there, inspired by a new place, painting the food he ate and the same ocean vistas I was admiring. Place has played such an important role in the evolution of my artwork. Leaving New York for the woods took my work in a new aesthetic direction as I photographed dishes on fallen trees and patches of moss. Traveling the Mediterranean has inspired me to use shades of blue like the sea and incorporate patterns like the tiled buildings I fell in love with in Lisbon.

From France, we took the most beautiful train ride along the water, across the border into Italy. We stayed in both Genoa and Cinque Terre on the stunning Ligurian coast. This area has such a rich culinary tradition, much of which is based on regional ingredients grown on terraced mountains above the sea. Recipes like focaccia, salsa di noci (walnut sauce, see page 23), pesto alla genovese (see page 170), and the sweet Sciacchetrà wine (see page 48) were created centuries ago and live on both in homes and at restaurants. My family has recipes that have been passed down, but none that have survived hundreds of years—how amazing to grow up surrounded by such culinary history!

In Cinque Terre we took a wine tour hike through the terraced vineyards (see page 49) and made pasta from scratch with a local chef (see page 166). In Genoa we stayed in the historic district, which had some of the best wood-fired pizza I've ever tasted.

Sicily was wild and wonderful. We stayed in an eighteenth-century villa near Catania, and then in an apartment with an ocean view in Cefalù. Driving through Sicily was not the easiest, with the tiny mountain roads and very, very narrow city streets. But it was amazing to be able to really see the villages and landscapes between each city. I found the lush and vibrant agriculture quite inspiring. En route to Mount Etna (see page 226), we passed citrus orchards, olive groves, vineyards, vines of magenta bougainvillea, and huge cacti full of pink pears, and after returning to our apartment in Cefalù, I began to paint all of it, much of which is included in this book. The region is known for its honey and pistachio production and we did tastings of each along the way. We stopped on the side of the road to buy water and instead found a wine cellar where you could bring water bottles to fill up with their local wine (see page 245, bottom row, second from right). We had oceanfront meals, visited a farm (see page 196), and went swimming in the sea in December.

After Sicily, we flew to Lisbon. While Portugal is not technically on the Mediterranean, many of the same ingredients we'd been enjoying were grown there and I was anxious to see how they were used in Portuguese cooking. Plus, we'd been wanting to visit for years! Lisbon's urban landscape is colorful and gritty and beautiful; we loved it. For us, Portugal felt quite affordable (as did Barcelona), and we were happy to be back to getting around on foot. Many evenings, we would visit the market and pick up olives, bread, cheese, and a bottle of Vinho Verde ("green wine" which is not really green, but a young, slightly fizzy white wine) for dinner at home. My parents and brother met us there for a week, and it was fun to explore the city with them, visiting holiday markets decked out in twinkling lights.

Midway through our trip we decided to drive south to the Algarve region of Portugal. We stayed for a week in Lagos and liked it so much that we decided to stay for another week in the next town over, Praia da Luz. Traveling off-season meant that we could easily change our schedule, book an apartment a couple days before, and places were less crowded. Each day, we explored a different seaside village or beach, and the weather was beautiful. We went olive oil tasting near Faro (see pages 114 and 115), had lunch on the beach in Sagres, and watched the surfers at sunset in Aljezur.

We went back to Lisbon for New Year's and rented a big apartment in the neighborhood of Belém with some friends from back home. We rang in 2018 on the roof overlooking the Tagus River with espumante (Portuguese sparkling wine) and fireworks, while the kids slept downstairs. We stayed down the block from the famous Pastéis de Belém, a bakery that makes the traditional mini custard pies (well worth the long line). One of my favorite meals of the trip was a long, fancy lunch at a restaurant overlooking the river in Lisbon called Topo Belém (during which Ezra definitely watched a show on my phone).

We ended the trip in Madrid with a festive celebration for Día de los Reyes (Three Kings' Day), which included the customary King's Cake and a big parade. We also ate our weight in patatas bravas. Although we were sad the trip was ending, I was ready to come home.

Though subtle, things did feel different once we were back. It was a unique experience for our little family. Being together 24/7 for three months straight was far removed from our usual routine of office, studio, and preschool. Although there were hard moments, it strengthened our relationship as a couple, and spending so much time with our kids during such a sweet and developmentally important time was special. The boys were so small that they will likely not remember the trip, but I like to think that little things did sink in. A couple months after returning, we went to a family wedding in Baltimore, Maryland. When we got off the plane, Ezra asked, "What language do they speak here?" which made us smile. Max turned one while we were in Madrid and was just starting to speak. He still calls water agua. I was reminded that we don't really need so many clothes, toys, and general clutter. We did just fine with those two carry-on suitcases and valued our few possessions even more. Overall, I think the trip reinforced that as a family we aim to value experiences over things, so when the opportunity to visit a new place arises, I know we'll make every effort to go.

There's something about travel that changes you. Once you get out of your comfort zone and into someone else's culture and way of life, your mind is opened. And that sense of openness and understanding comes home with you, or at least it has with me.

I didn't buy many souvenirs, but I returned with new ideas, new recipes, and a revitalized view of my life at home. One of the resounding lessons I've brought back is the importance of slowing down to enjoy my meals. In Barcelona, no one took their coffee to go, but instead enjoyed it at the bar each morning next to other neighbors on their way to work. In Genoa, our favorite lunch spot was packed with locals enjoying a nice meal in the middle of their workday. In all of the countries we visited, the culture insists upon coming together, sitting down, and appreciating the food and conversation. And so, by creating this book, my hope is to bring home a little bit of that magic, encouraging us all to embrace this kind of pause and gratitude for gathering together with good food, wherever in the world we might be.

Happy travels!

Erin

For trip resources and more photos visit www.theforestfeast.com and follow along @theforestfeast. Tag recipes you make from this book #forestfeastmediterranean.

tips for using this book

RECIPES serve 4-6
unless otherwise noted

MEASUREMENTS

T	tablespoon
t	teaspoon
C	cup
kg	kilogram
g	gram
cm	centimeter
mm	millimeter
in	inch
L	liter
ml	milliliter

With these recipes I hope to inspire you to experience some of the traditions we came to enjoy so much in Europe around eating and drinking. We often had an apéritif, a before-dinner drink (such as the one on page 50), with some snacks to whet the appetite, and a digestif, an after-dinner drink (such as the one on page 60), to aid in digestion and enjoyably lengthen the end of the meal.

Overall, the dishes in this book are small plates and sides that are meant to be shared around the table. You could serve a couple of them as appetizers at a cocktail party or several of them on a buffet as a meal. In Spain especially, I loved the idea that tapas and small bites could be enjoyed during the day or even late night.

SALT { I use coarse or kosher salt when cooking & flaky Maldon sea salt to serve.

For good-quality olive oil I prefer California Olive Ranch.

Praia da Luz, Portugal

Girona, Spain

Itinerary
our 3-month journey

1. BARCELONA, SPAIN: 1 month. Side/day trips to Girona, Sitges, Besalú, Costa Brava.

2. ANTIBES, FRANCE: 1 week. We flew from Barcelona to Nice. Day trips to Nice, Cannes, Èze, and Saint-Paul-de-Vence.

3. LIGURIA, ITALY: 1 week. We took a stunning train ride along the coast from Nice to Genoa. We got pesto pasta immediately upon arrival, followed by focaccia and gelato. In nearby Cinque Terre, we stayed in Monterosso al Mare and hiked between these idyllic seaside towns.

4. SICILY, ITALY: 1 week. We flew from Genoa into Catania and out of Palermo and explored in between by car.

5. LISBON, PORTUGAL: 2 weeks. We stayed first in the downtown area and then in Belém.

6. THE ALGARVE REGION, PORTUGAL: We intended to stay for 1 week but liked it so much we stayed for 2. We drove from Lisbon and stayed in Lagos and Praia da Luz and explored many towns nearby including Tavira, Salema, and Sagres.

7. MADRID, SPAIN: 1 week. We flew from Lisbon to Madrid and spent our last days back in Spain eating tapas before flying back to San Francisco.

Here & opposite: Èze, France

Antibes, France

SNACKS

The quality of the produce blew us away in France. The farmers' market was around the corner from where we stayed in Antibes. We visited daily to pick up the best cheeses and vegetables for crudités. We kept returning for these radishes, which were so delicious with butter and an apéritif at home before walking to dinner.

Sauces, etc.

CHILI OIL:

Simply put 2 T dried red pepper flakes into a jar with 1 c (240 ml) olive oil. Seal & gently shake to mix, then let sit for about 3 days or until the oil starts to become red. It will last a couple weeks, but does get progressively spicier! I love this on pizza and pretty much everything else. We saw it in restaurants in both Italy & Portugal.

BASIL OIL:

Process ¾ c (180 ml) olive oil & ¼ c (10 g) basil leaves in the blender until smooth. In France we saw this drizzled on a bowl of olives, which was delicious. It's also great to dip bread in, spread on sandwiches, or drizzle over salad or vegetables.

LEMON-PARMESAN VINAIGRETTE:

Using an immersion blender, blend the juice from 1 lemon (about 2 T) with ⅓ c (80 ml) olive oil, 2 T finely grated Parmesan & a pinch of salt & pepper. You can also shake this in a jar, but stir right before using. It's a bright & tangy salad dressing inspired by the abundance of citrus we saw growing all over Italy.

MINT-PEA DIP:

In the food processor, mix 1 (16 oz/454 g) bag frozen peas (defrosted), juice from ½ lemon, 1 c (50 g) mint (a few stems are OK), ½ c (120 ml) olive oil, 1 clove garlic & a pinch of salt. Blend until very creamy. Enjoy with crudités (page 26), on bread, or with crackers.

WALNUT DIP/SAUCE:

In the cooking class I took in Italy (page 166), I learned how to make a typical Ligurian walnut sauce (salsa di noci) for pasta, but I also like it as a dip. Blend ½ c (50 g) whole walnuts, 3 T ricotta, 1 t lemon juice, 1 T fresh marjoram leaves, 1 clove garlic, 2 T olive oil, ¼ c (60 ml) water, salt & pepper. Use as is for a dip with crudités (page 26), or heat it & thin it out with a splash of water for a creamy pasta sauce.

ROMESCO SAUCE:

I got the most lovely plate of roasted vegetables with this sauce while sitting outdoors in the Gothic Quarter of Barcelona & I fell in love (see page 30). It's nutty & tangy & great on pretty much everything. In a food processor or blender, mix 6 oz (170 g) roasted red peppers from a jar (drained), 1 plum tomato (cubed), ¼ c (35 g) roasted almonds, ¼ c (60 ml) olive oil, 2 cloves garlic, juice from ½ lemon, 1 day-old heel or slice of rustic bread (ripped), a pinch of paprika, salt & pepper. I like to pulse while processing to give it a more rustic texture that is not super smooth.

PISTACHIO PESTO:

While in Italy, we visited Genoa (known for its pesto) & Sicily (known for its pistachios) & this is my ode to them both! I use a food processor, which maintains some of the nutty texture, which I like. Blend together 2 c (80 g) basil leaves (loosely packed), 2 chopped scallions, 3 cloves garlic, ⅓ c (30 g) grated Parmesan, ½ c (65 g) pistachios (shelled & roasted), zest from 1 lime & ¾ c (180 ml) olive oil. Try it with the pasta on page 170.

In each country we visited, our meals often started with a bowl of olives. The olives were usually local and quite fresh. Restaurants seemed to have their own unique way of curing them, so that the taste was just slightly different in each place. During our first meal in Lisbon, we were served a bowl of olives that had fresh garlic slices mixed in, and I loved the simple, flavor-packed combination, perfect with a cocktail. Restaurants in Barcelona added citrus, peppers, or herbs. One restaurant in France served theirs mixed with a basil oil (page 22) they made themselves. I kept seeing special olive serving bowls in Portuguese restaurants with a separate compartment for the pits, and I was happy to pick this one (at right) up at a little shop in Sintra. Alternatively, you can set out a small ramekin for the pits.

dressed-up OLIVES

1. Buy 1 c (225 g) of olives. I find the best ones are in the deli section of my grocery store. You can buy mixed olives or just one type, but choose ones that contain pits. I like a mix of green & purple olives in my bowl.

2. Mix the olives in a shallow bowl with 2 chopped cloves garlic & a drizzle of olive oil. Grate some orange zest over the top of the bowl & sprinkle on a few fresh thyme leaves. Serve with drinks before dinner.

Moorish Castle,
Sintra, Portugal

Crudités PLATTER

A colorful crudités platter or board is a great appetizer to start any gathering. Crudités means "raw things" in French, and one typically consists of raw vegetables with dip, but you can also add nuts, olives, fruit, cheese, breadsticks, or crackers to make it a heartier spread. I like to collect as many "mini" vegetables as I can find, in as many colors as possible. Serve it with your favorite dip or dressing or try my Walnut Dip on page 23.

1 watermelon radish I use a mandoline to slice it very thinly

¼ head purple cauliflower cut into florets

2 heads endive yellow or purple, leaves peeled apart

4 mini cucumbers keep peel on, quarter lengthwise

8 mini carrots peeled & stems trimmed

1 c (145g) cherry tomatoes mix of yellow & red

12 mini peppers sweet peppers—yellow, orange & red

On a large platter or cutting board, arrange the vegetables around the dip by color. Other ideas: red radishes, bell pepper slices, broccoli, snap peas, green beans, celery, jicama, asparagus & mandoline-sliced beets.

Burst Tomatoes
& TORN MOZZARELLA

They sold the most beautiful and fragrant vines of cherry tomatoes at the farmers' market in Antibes, France (see page 20), which inspired this recipe.

Roast 2 vines of *cherry tomatoes* (about 20 tomatoes) on a baking sheet with olive oil & salt at 375°F (190°C) for 15-20 min or until the tomatoes have burst a bit but are not dried out.

Carefully place the cooked tomatoes on a platter alongside 4 oz (115 g) fresh *mozzarella* that has been torn into pieces. Sprinkle the whole platter with capers, lemon zest, flaky salt, black pepper & lots of olive oil.

Serve alongside slices of grilled or pan-fried *sourdough bread* that has been brushed with olive oil.

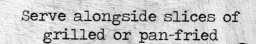

PINTXOS

On a fun night in Barcelona, we went pintxos bar-hopping. Originating in northern Spain, pintxos (in Basque) or pinchos (in Spanish) are appetizers on long toothpicks. In the Poble Sec neighborhood, our favorite stop was the very crowded La Tasqueta de Blai. There are trays and trays of pintxos all along the bar, and you just grab the ones you want and return to your table. Most were about 1 euro, but some were more, depending on the ingredients. You keep track of your toothpicks (pricier ones had different colored toothpicks), and they charge you by counting them at the end.

Make your own pintxos at home by piling ingredients on top of sliced baguette. Here are some flavor combinations inspired by what we tasted in Spain.

pesto (store-bought or page 23), roasted red pepper (from a jar), mozzarella ball & balsamic glaze (store-bought or just balsamic vinegar)

fig jam & a brie wedge that has been pressed into pine nuts

a small wedge of Tortilla Española (page 156) & 2 cherry tomatoes

caramelized onions (thinly sliced & cooked with olive oil about 30 min in a pan on low) topped with apple slices & fresh thyme leaves

Romesco sauce (page 23 or store-bought marinara), ½ fried egg & a Padrón (or shishito) pepper that's been briefly fried in olive oil on med/high until it blisters.

creamy goat cheese (chèvre), blackberry jam, walnut pieces & a basil leaf

Drinks in Spain were often served with something pickled, like these "banderilla" tapas mounted on a long toothpick. We got so many delicious ideas for skewered tapas in Barcelona (see Pintxos, page 30), but I love the simplicity of this one, and that a platter of them can be made well in advance. For this appetizer, you can buy jars of various pickled items or make your own (see page 40).

BANDERILLAS

On a long toothpick or short skewer, stack a variety of pickled items, including:

- cornichons
- red peppers
- carrots
- olives
- jalapeños
- pearl onions

Plaça Reial, Barcelona, Spain

Especially in northern Spain, it's common to see a small appetizer served on one skewer or toothpick (see Pintxos, page 30 and Banderillas, page 32). I saw a deviled egg served like this at a bar in Barcelona and loved having additional flavors like radish and olive "packaged" with it.

GARLICKY Deviled Egg SKEWERS

1. cut 6 hard-boiled eggs in half lengthwise & remove yolks

2. mash the yolks in a bowl with: — 3 T mayonnaise — 2 minced cloves garlic

3. spoon the mixture into the egg white halves & sprinkle with red pepper flakes

4. using a 4-in (10-cm) toothpick/skewer, first thread a radish slice, then a garlic-stuffed olive, then the deviled egg, then another radish slice on the bottom to keep the stack from tipping over (you'll need about 6 radishes & 12 olives)

Park Güell, Barcelona, Spain

I found these adorable mini red cherry peppers in the deli section of my supermarket, near the olives, but they can also come in a jar. Look for the pickled, sweet variety of pimiento that has been destemmed and deseeded.

STUFFED
cherry peppers

¼ c (30 g) goat cheese

¼ c (60 g) cream cheese

} Bring both to room temperature & mix.

Pipe or spoon the cheese mixture into

12 pickled cherry peppers.

Put them all on a plate & sprinkle with:

- lemon zest
- chopped chives
- pepper

We often saw this typical Italian antipasto on menus in Sicily. It's a versatile dish that can easily be made in advance and is great to have on hand. It can be served as an appetizer or to enhance a main course, scoops of it can be served on toasted bread, mixed into pasta, over creamy polenta, or even alongside eggs. It keeps well & some think it's even better on the second day.

CAPONATA

serves 6-8 as an appetizer

① cut 1 eggplant & 1 onion into ½-in (12-mm) cubes

② put the cubes in a big skillet along with 4 minced cloves garlic, a generous amount of olive oil (start with ¼ c/60 ml) & a pinch of salt & pepper

③ Cook for 15-20 min on medium heat, stirring often. Then add 3 diced Roma tomatoes, 3 T red wine vinegar, 2 T capers, 1 T honey & a bit more salt & pepper. Cook for another 10 min, stirring often. Transfer to a bowl & garnish with pine nuts & basil.

Aci Castello, Sicily

Charcuterie (very thinly sliced preserved meats), often in combination with bread and cheese, are a common way to start a meal in the countries we visited. I thought it'd be fun to do a colorful vegetarian platter inspired by this idea and "preserve" some of the vegetables with a quick pickling.

VEGETABLE *Charcuterie* PLATTER

Arrange all the items on a large cutting board with a small knife for the cheese & breadsticks. Garnish the platter with fresh herb sprigs like rosemary or thyme. Set out a few store-bought dips like olive tapenade, mustard, or hummus, plus some sun-dried tomatoes & olives.

→ **2 golden beets**

use a mandoline to slice them into very thin rounds

→ **1 watermelon radish**

use a mandoline to slice it into very thin rounds

→ **15 stalks asparagus**

Trim the stalk ends & steam them for 2 or 3 min in a covered skillet with a little water, just until they are bright green. Allow to cool.

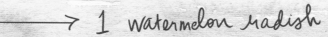

→ **2 carrots**

Look for big ones & use a peeler to make long ribbons. Press hard to make the ribbons a little thicker.

→ **8 oz (225g) cheese**

I bought very thinly sliced Havarti & Swiss to wrap around the steamed asparagus. In addition, include a small round of creamy cheese like Brie that can be spread on the beet & radish slices like crackers.

FOR THE PICKLING:

Boil 1 c (240 ml) water, 1 c (240 ml) apple cider vinegar & 1 T kosher salt. Simmer a couple minutes, until salt dissolves. Allow to cool, then soak the beet & carrot slices in the liquid for at least 1 hour in the refrigerator. Pat dry before serving.

While staying in the Algarve region of southern Portugal, we'd often take drinks and snacks to the beach for happy hour in the evening. Most grocery stores sold boxes of fancy dried figs stuffed with Marcona almonds, which were easy to pack and great with a drink before dinner. It's an even better combination when you add cheese.

Stuffed Dried Figs

12 dried figs ⟶

Look for the type that is light in color, flat & round, such as Turkish figs. Remove the stems & slice them almost all the way in half, but leave one side partially attached, like a clamshell.

3 oz (85g) goat cheese
12 walnut halves }

Look for a soft goat cheese, like chèvre, & roll it into marble-sized balls. Place 1 marble inside each "clamshell" along with a walnut half.

Alternatively, like we saw in the stores, you can cut the fig all the way in half & press a few Marcona almonds in around the edges of one half, like the petals of a flower. Place the other fig half on top & press together like a little sandwich.

Praia da Salema, Portugal

Praia da Luz, Portugal

The Black Anchor, Tavira, Portugal

Tavira, Portugal

Potato chips, lupini beans
and olives were served wi[th]
our Aperol spritzes in
Portovenere, Italy

DRINKS

clockwise from top left: Aperol spritzes on the beach in Monterosso al Mare, Italy; sipping local wine at Ananasso Bar in Vernazza, Italy; Monterosso al Mare, Italy; grapes drying in Cinque Terre, Italy, to make the regional dessert wine called Sciacchetrà

In Cinque Terre, at the end of a wine tour
hike we sampled the work of local winemaker
Luciano Capellini with some focaccia from a
nearby bakery (for more info see page 243)

This trendy yet classic Italian aperitif might be enjoyed on a warm afternoon by the beach or before a meal. Aperol, a bright orange bitter liqueur that's similar to Campari but has a lower alcohol content, is mixed with prosecco for this drink. The traditional recipe often includes just a splash of soda and an orange slice for garnish, but my twist offers a bit more fizz and the refreshing aroma of grapefruit and thyme with each sip.

SERVES 1

grapefruit & thyme
APEROL
SPRITZ

Aperol
Prosecco
seltzer

pour equal parts
(about 2 oz/60 ml each)
over a glass of ice

Look for unsweetened grapefruit-flavored
seltzer like (pamplemousse-flavored)
La Croix & if you can't find prosecco,
any dry sparkling white wine will work.

GARNISH

a slice of pink grapefruit & 2 sprigs of fresh thyme

In Spain, this warm-weather drink is typically an even mix of red table wine and lemon soda (like Fanta) with a lemon slice for garnish. It is similar to sangria, but more basic with less fruit. My version is a little lighter, using an unsweetened lemon-flavored seltzer, but it goes down just as easily. Any red wine will do, but I prefer something full-bodied, like Tempranillo.

strawberry
TINTO DE VERANO

Pour equal parts over a glass of ice:

{ red wine
{ lemon seltzer

↓

Add a squeeze of lemon
(about 1 t),
halved strawberries on a
skewer & a lemon slice as
garnish.

STIR.

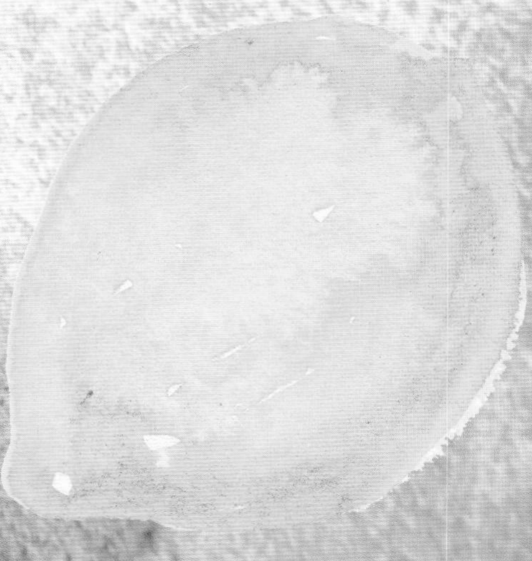

GIN & TONIC BAR

Serves 1

{ 2 oz (60ml) gin
½ c (120ml) tonic
ice

Gin & tonics served in giant goblet glasses were very popular in Barcelona when we were visiting. There was a bar on our corner called Xixbar Gin & Cocktails that made all different types. I had one there with cloves that was delicious and perfect for colder weather. If you're having people over for drinks, make a platter with several different garnish options and allow guests to build their own G&T. I like to fill the glass about halfway with ice, then add a 1:2 ratio of gin to tonic, followed by 2 or 3 of the garnishes below. Keep in mind the garnish is mostly about enhancing the sensory experience with aroma and not necessarily to eat.

thyme

rosemary

mint

cucumber

clementine wheel

orange twist

lemon wedge

lime wheel

pink grapefruit slice

pink peppercorn

dried juniper berries

cloves

additional garnish options: blackberries, edible flowers (like nasturtium), star anise, cinnamon sticks, fresh ginger slices, jalapeños, basil, lavender, and pomegranate seeds

Garnish combination ideas
(clockwise from top left):
•Blackberry & Grapefruit
•Clementine & Nasturtium
•Orange & Cloves
•Rosemary & Pink Peppercorns

55

CAVA Sangria

On warm fall evenings in Barcelona, we would sit at outdoor cafes to have a drink & tapas while Ezra played in the plaza. Our favorite neighborhood spot served a delicious white cava sangria. Cava is a Spanish white sparkling wine (similar to France's Champagne or Italy's prosecco).

1 bottle (750 ml) **CAVA** or any dry sparkling white wine

2 c (480 ml) WHITE GRAPE JUICE

Mix in a pitcher with:

1 c (165 g) strawberries cut in circles

1 c (125 g) raspberries

½ grapefruit, cut into triangles (peel on)

Serve chilled or over ice.

Lavender grows abundantly in southern France, and I loved seeing big dried bunches of it for sale at the farmers' market in Antibes, just steps from where we stayed.

Lavender LEMONADE

①.
In a pitcher, steep 2 lavender tea bags in 2 c (480 ml) hot water for 5 min.

②.
Remove the tea bags & stir in 3 T agave or honey until dissolved.

③.
Add 2 c (480 ml) cold water & juice from 4 lemons (about ½ c/120 ml). Stir.

④.
Allow to cool, then pour over ice & garnish with lemon slices & sprigs of culinary lavender. Add more agave if you wish.

Port is typically a sweet dessert wine or digestif that comes from the Douro Valley of northern Portugal. It's often enjoyed after dinner on its own, but it can also be mixed into cocktails. This recipe is inspired by the cherry liqueur Ginjinha, served in mini chocolate cups, that we tasted at the festive outdoor Christmas market in Praça do Rossio in Lisbon.

cherry-Port COCKTAIL

serves 1

In a cocktail shaker,
shake the following with ice:

2 oz (60 ml) ruby Port

1 oz (30 ml) whiskey

dash bitters

Pour into a glass & garnish with
3 Luxardo maraschino cherries

Boat ride to see the
grottoes in Lagos, Portugal

blood orange
VERMOUTH COCKTAIL
serves 1

POUR OVER A GLASS OF ICE:

- 6 oz (180 ml) sweet red vermouth
- a dash of bitters
- a splash of soda

Stir & then add 1 large green olive on a toothpick & a slice of blood orange.

After a few days in Spain, I noticed that people around me at cafes were all ordering a red drink I didn't recognize. I asked a server what it was and he answered, "vermut." Just vermouth, I thought? Straight? I'm used to seeing it mixed into cocktails, but in Spain I quickly learned to love it on the rocks as an apéritif. Some places also throw in soda and bitters, and the garnish is usually orange, but it varies. It's a drink that is typically enjoyed on Sunday afternoons, perhaps the way I might drink a Bloody Mary.

Vermouth on our balcony in Barcelona

We spent warm evenings
in Barcelona having
drinks & tapas in
different plazas while
Ezra played outdoors

The olive oil shop
& restaurant Deli'
in Èze, France

We sipped vermouth
outside on a
Sunday afternoon
at Café Flanders
in Barcelona

Bar Cin Cin,
Castelbuono,
Sicily

Restaurante Chico Zé,
Faro, Portugal

SALADS

ARANCE LOCALI
SICILIA Kg5 €4.00

Sicily

The Algarve, Portugal

In every country we visited, we saw orchards bursting with oranges, which inspired this recipe. I also like this salad because it does quite well when made in advance (however, add the basil just before serving).

golden BEET & ORANGE salad

Peel 5 large golden beets & cut into 1-in (2½-cm) cubes.
Boil in salted water for 5-7 min, until slightly tender.
Strain & run under cold water to cool. Toss the beets in
a bowl with 2 peeled, cubed oranges, 2 T chopped basil,
2 T sliced red onion, 1 T olive oil, salt & pepper.

Barcelona, Spain

Tile backdrop from Gaudí's benches
at Park Güell, Barcelona, Spain

seared FENNEL & clementine SALAD

The idyllic village of Saint-Paul-de-Vence is one of the oldest medieval towns on the French Riviera. I loved wandering the cobblestone streets and seeing the abundance of citrus that grows there.

cut

2 fennel bulbs — tops removed & set aside

5 clementines — peel 4 of them & slice into rounds

2 T Kalamata olives — whole, pitted

1 T mint — chopped

red onion — rings from 1 or 2 round center slices

Slice the fennel bulbs very thinly, keeping some pieces in large slabs. Sauté in 1-2 T olive oil & a pinch of salt on med heat until just a bit tender & golden on both sides (about 5 min), then spread out on a platter. Top with the clementine rounds, olives, mint, onion rings & a few small fennel fronds. Halve the last clementine & squeeze the juice over the whole platter along with a sprinkle of olive oil, salt & pepper.

Saint-Paul-de-Vence, France

FRIED Lentil Salad

One of my favorite outdoor lunches was on a Sunday afternoon after visiting Gaudi's stunning Park Güell in Barcelona. We stumbled upon the prettiest plaza on our walk home and sat down at Café Flanders for a bite. While the warm afternoon light beamed through fall-colored leaves, we sipped vermouth alongside locals and got several small dishes to share, one of which was a salad topped with fried onions and lentils.

1. Thinly slice 1 large onion. Sauté on med/low in a generous amount of olive oil (about 3 T, ¼ t paprika & a pinch of salt & pepper until golden, stirring occasionally, about 15 min.

2. Add a 15-oz (425-g) can drained lentils to the pan, plus 1 c (160 g) halved cherry tomatoes. Sauté 3 min.

3. Dress 2 handfuls baby kale with olive oil & a squeeze of lemon. Lay kale out on a platter.

4. Spoon the warm lentil mixture over the kale then season the platter with a bit more lemon juice plus a pinch of salt, pepper & paprika. Enjoy warm.

Avocado & Bean Salad

serves 4

6 oz (170 g) shelled, cooked
EDAMAME BEANS

1 (15-oz/425-g) can
drained, rinsed
BUTTER BEANS

TOSS
the beans in a bowl with
a bit of olive oil,
juice from ½ lemon,
1 T chopped fresh oregano,
salt & pepper.

SPREAD
the bean mixture out on a platter &
top with cubes from 1 avocado
& 2 hard- or soft-boiled eggs
cut in quarters.

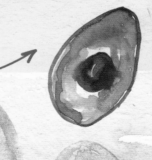

SPRINKLE
the platter with a bit more olive oil,
salt & pepper before serving.

WARM
goat cheese
& FIG SALAD

During lunch at Le Tilleul in Saint-Paul-de-Vence, France (see page 163), we sat outside, drank rosé, and had a goat cheese salad with a unique presentation. Each piece of cheese on top was wrapped in a crispy dough, making it both filling and delicious. You can use any vinaigrette, or mine on page 22.

phyllo dough   you'll need less than half of a 16-oz (455-g) box

goat Brie   a 6 oz (180 g) round, cut into 8 small pieces

mixed greens   3 handfuls (about 4 oz/115 g) tossed in vinaigrette

dried figs   8 figs cut in rounds, stems removed

walnuts   roasted & salted, ⅓ c (40 g) chopped

1. Stack 3 sheets of phyllo dough & cut it into 8 (5-in/12-cm) squares. Place a small wedge (about 1 in/2½-cm) of goat Brie on each square & wrap each up like a little gift, using olive oil on your fingers to seal the edges. Place them fold-side down on a baking sheet & rub a bit more oil on top of each. Bake at 375°F (190°C) for 10–12 min, until golden. If cheese leaks out, once cooled, break it off & add it to the salad.

2. On a platter, place the warm cheese "packages" on a bed of dressed salad greens. Top the platter with the dried fig & walnut pieces, plus some freshly ground black pepper.

Provençal Potato Salad

cut-----

3 c (420g) halved mini potatoes

Boil 10 min or until fork-tender. Rinse under cold water to cool.

TOSS WITH:
¼ red onion, diced
3 T capers
1 T grainy mustard
2 T chopped parsley
1 T olive oil
salt & pepper to taste

Antibes, France

Pesto is from the region of Liguria, Italy, that we visited and it is not only for pasta! I also love it as a dressing on salads.

PESTO chopped SALAD

1 ear corn, kernels removed
1 English cucumber, peel on, cubed
½ c (60 g) chopped roasted walnuts
¼ c (40 g) pitted Kalamata olives, chopped
1 green bell pepper, cubed
¼ red onion, diced

Toss all ingredients in a bowl

with 3 T store-bought pesto or the Pistachio Pesto on page 23. Enjoy chilled or at room temp.

Pesto originates in Genoa, Italy (below). During the colder months when you don't have fresh tomatoes and herbs on hand, try this tasty adaptation of the classic Italian salad. I get many of my plates at antique sales, but the plate on the right is part of a set of hand-painted dishes my grandmother bought in Italy decades ago and gave to me recently.

Winter Caprese

1. Slice 8 oz (225 g) fresh mozzarella cheese into rounds.

2. Cut 4 beets into ¼-inch (6-mm) rounds (no need to peel). Look for beets that are a similar size in diameter to your mozzarella.

3. Lay the beet slices out on a baking sheet & drizzle with olive oil, salt & pepper. Roast for 25 min at 400°F (205°C), until fork-tender with a few crispy edges.

4. Lay the cheese & beet slices on a large plate in a circular pattern, overlapping each just a bit. Sprinkle with olive oil, salt & pepper & put a dollop of pesto in the middle. Enjoy cold or at room temperature.

cucumber carpaccio

Use a mandoline (or a knife) to very thinly slice 1 large English cucumber into rounds (peel on). Fan the slices out on a round platter or large plate, overlapping the edges of each slice a bit. Start at the edges of the platter & move inward. Start a second layer on the outer edge if necessary to fit all the pieces.

Sprinkle over the cucumber {
pine nuts
fresh dill
golden raisins
chopped pistachios
lemon juice
olive oil
salt & pepper

Shaved SNAP PEA Salad

you'll need:

3 c (185 g) snap peas (about 2 big handfuls, ends trimmed)
2 T finely grated Parmesan
3 T pine nuts
6 dates, pitted & diced
2 T chopped mint
1 T olive oil
2 t lemon juice
black pepper

Cut the snap peas diagonally as thinly as possible. This is easy but does take a bit of time. A sharp knife helps.

Toss all the ingredients in a mixing bowl & enjoy chilled or at room temp.

GREENS & GRAINS
with roasted carrots

cut ovals

Diagonally slice 4 carrots & lay them on a baking sheet. Sprinkle with olive oil, garlic powder, red pepper flakes, salt & pepper. Roast at 425°F (220°C) for 20 min or until crispy around the edges.

Meanwhile, fry 1 c (197 g) cooked rice (or any leftover grain) in a pan on med heat with olive oil for 3 min or until some crispy bits form (I like to use a mix of quinoa & wild rice). Allow both the rice & carrots to cool for a min, then toss with 3 handfuls fresh salad greens & your favorite vinaigrette, or mine on page 22.

Algarve Salad

This salad is inspired by one we had at Restaurante Raposo on the beach in Sagres, Portugal. So many dishes in Portugal incorporated dried oregano and it was sold in big bunches on the stem at the markets, as pictured at right.

½ green bell pepper

½ red bell pepper

handful cherry tomatoes

1 can (15 oz / 430 g) chickpeas (drained)

1 cucumber

handful pitted kalamata olives

2 hard-boiled eggs

Cube the peppers, tomatoes & cucumber. Toss all ingredients (except eggs) in a bowl with a splash of olive oil, rice vinegar, salt & pepper. Quarter the eggs lengthwise & arrange them around the edges. Sprinkle dried or fresh oregano on top.

photo of dish at right taken in Praia da Luz, Portugal →

QUINOA FRUIT SALAD

1 c
(160 g) ← Cantaloupe, cubed

{ Grapes, halved

small
handful ← { raspberries
each

{ blackberries

{ strawberries, cubed

3 T ← cooked quinoa

1 T ← fresh mint

Toss all ingredients. Spread out in a shallow bowl &
very lightly drizzle with olive oil before serving.

POMEGRANATE
stuffed avocados

serves 4

for the filling

CHERRY TOMATOES ½ c (75 g) diced

MOZZARELLA PEARLS ½ c (40 g) (or diced fresh mozzarella)

POMEGRANATE SEEDS ¼ c (35 g)

plus a bit of olive oil, salt & pepper

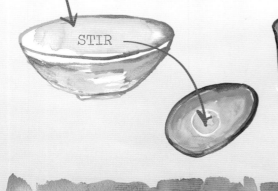

STIR

Halve 2 avocados lengthwise &
remove the pits. Spoon the filling
into each. Serve them with spoons,
each drizzled with a bit more olive
oil, salt & pepper. Serve any leftover
filling in a separate bowl. The
stuffed avocados can also be served
on a bed of dressed greens.

Lisbon, Portugal

While staying in the beautiful seaside village of Praia da Luz, Portugal, over Christmas, we explored a different beach town each day. The weather was beautiful, and we'd often sit at a cafe on the water for lunch. One dish we kept seeing on menus was a chickpea and cod salad, and this is my vegetarian adaptation of it.

CHICKPEA & TORN MOZZARELLA SALAD

1 (15 oz/430 g) can chickpeas, drained
6 oz (170 g) fresh mozzarella, torn into pieces
2 scallions, chopped
3 T diced red onion
1 T chopped fresh parsley
zest from 1 lemon
juice from ½ lemon
1 T olive oil
salt & pepper to taste

Mix all the ingredients in a bowl & serve alongside
additional lemon wedges, salt & pepper.
Best enjoyed outdoors!

Praia da Luz, Portugal

SPICY Melon Salad

on a platter...

① spread out a small handful of arugula, then cover it with:

- ¼ honeydew, sliced in thin crescents
- ¼ cantaloupe, sliced in thin crescents
- 1 red tomato, sliced in rounds
- 1 yellow tomato, sliced in rounds

②. then sprinkle on top...

↳ fresh arugula, olive oil, flaky salt & red pepper flakes

✴ If you have spicy oil on hand (page 22) sprinkle that instead, sparingly ✴

Santa Maria La Scala, Sicily

roasted CAULIFLOWER Salad

① SPREAD
out florets from 1 head of cauliflower with 1 sliced onion on a baking sheet.

② SPRINKLE
the whole baking sheet with

{
olive oil   about 2 T
garlic   2 cloves, minced
red pepper flakes   about ¼ t
cinnamon   about ¼ t
cumin   about ¼ t
salt & pepper   to taste

③ ROAST at 425°F (220°C) for 30 min

④ TOSS
the cooked cauliflower & onions in a bowl with ¼ c (35 g) pine nuts & ¼ c (35 g) raisins. Serve at room temp with a dollop of Greek yogurt & a lemon wedge per person.

I think the dishes we tasted in the Mediterranean region were so good because they used seasonal produce that was grown nearby and recently picked. This salad is best made during the warmer months when your farmers' markets are selling in-season peaches, corn, and tomatoes.

Summer Corn & Peach Salad

Toss in a bowl:

2 peaches, cut into small cubes
2 ears of corn, kernels cut off
1 c (145 g) halved yellow cherry tomatoes
1 small orange bell pepper, diced
¼ red onion, diced
2 T chopped basil
2 T chopped mint
1 T olive oil
2 t red wine vinegar

Serve in a bowl or on a platter topped with 2 T grated Parmesan & a sprinkling of black pepper.

Le Jardin Exotique, Èze, France

Italian
WILD RICE
Salad

cooked wild rice — 3 c (432 g)

Cherry tomatoes — ⅔ c (95 g) halved yellow & red

marinated artichoke hearts — 5 pieces from a jar, sliced (about 4 T)

sun-dried tomatoes — about 2 T chopped from a jar (in oil, drained)

Capers — 2 T from a jar (drained)

red onion — ¼ c (30 g) diced

Italian parsley — ⅓ c (17 g) chopped (loosely packed)

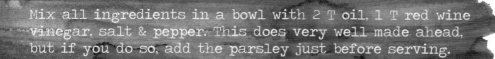

Mix all ingredients in a bowl with 2 T oil, 1 T red wine vinegar, salt & pepper. This does very well made ahead, but if you do so, add the parsley just before serving.

Aci Castello, Sicily

FARRO-CUCUMBER SALAD

1 c (200 g) dry farro

1 cucumber skin on, cubed

3 T parsley roughly chopped

½ c (75 g) feta crumbled

½ c (60 g) walnuts chopped

Bring a pot of water to a boil then add the farro. Depending on grain size, farro can have different cooking times anywhere from 10-30 min. I boil the farro like pasta & taste it after 10 min to see if it is al dente & a bit chewy yet. When done, strain excess water & run under cold water to cool. Toss the cooked farro in a mixing bowl with all the other ingredients, plus juice & zest from ½ lemon, 2 T olive oil, salt & pepper to taste.

here: Lisbon
right: the Algarve, Portugal
bottom left & right: Lagos, Portugal

artichokes & citrus
at a market in Sicily

BLETTE
CHOU VERT
Carottes
Navets
OIGNONS
5,90 € le Kg
agrinat
Antibes, France

SMALL PLATES

When we were in southern Portugal, we visited
the groves and production site of Monterosa
Extra-Virgin Olive Oil (here & opposite) in
Moncarapacho and did a tasting of several of
their artisan varieties. I learned so much, and
it reinforced what a difference high-quality
olive oil can make in the flavor of a dish.

Most evenings in Barcelona, we took a walk to a nearby plaza where we would sit at an outdoor cafe to enjoy patatas bravas and a drink while the kids played. On more traditional menus, this was sometimes one of the only vegetarian options, so we ordered them often, perhaps even daily. They are usually just regular potato cubes that are probably deep-fried, but my adaptation includes sweet potatoes and is baked. The magic is in the sauce, which was sometimes on top, sometimes on the side. Sometimes there was also a white creamy sauce in addition to the red sauce, and sometimes the two seeemed to be combined. You can leave out the sriracha in my sauce recipe if you (or your kids) don't like it spicy.

Patatas Bravas

Cube the potatoes into 1-in (2½-cm) pieces & spread out on a baking sheet with plenty of olive oil (at least 2 T) & a couple pinches of salt. Use your hands & toss to coat.

{ 2 waxy potatoes I use Yukon Gold
{ 2 small sweet potatoes

no need to peel

Roast at 425°F (220°C) for 40-45 min

Stir them a few times while they're baking so that they get golden on all sides. Add a bit more oil if they are sticking.

FOR THE SAUCE:

Sauté ½ large onion (chopped) & 2 cloves garlic in 1 T olive oil on med/low until golden, about 10 min. Use an immersion blender to blend the onion mixture with 3 T mayo, 3 T tomato paste, 1 t sriracha & ½ t smoky paprika. Serve the sauce in a dish on the side, with toothpicks or forks for dipping.

Paella, a rice dish often made with seafood, is perhaps one of the most well-known Spanish dishes. It is typically served family style, in a special pan that it is cooked in. While in Barcelona, we tried a few vegetarian versions. In the Barceloneta neighborhood by the beach, we ordered a carrot and red pepper paella. But I think my favorite was one made at a little stall in the back of the bustling Boqueria market off Las Ramblas that had a medley of peas. The rice in paella is traditionally turned a golden yellow using saffron, but I opted for a more readily available and affordable spice, turmeric.

Snap Pea Paella

① 3 c (720 ml) vegetable broth
1½ c (285 g) Arborio rice

In a pot bring the broth to a boil, then add the rice & simmer, covered, for about 20 min, until the broth has been absorbed & the rice is cooked. Taste the rice & if it's too al dente, simmer a couple more min with an extra splash of broth.

When the rice is done, stir in:

2 t turmeric
½ t garlic powder
salt + pepper

② In a separate pan, sauté 2 c (120 g) SNAP PEAS (ends trimmed) & 3 chopped SCALLIONS with 1 T olive oil for 1 min, or until the peas are bright green. Turn the heat off & add the cooked rice plus another 1 T olive oil. Stir.

③ Spread the rice mixture out on a platter & sprinkle with fresh chopped flat-leaf PARSLEY. Season with salt & pepper.

We had a creative vegetarian meal at Galleria Ristorante in Cefalù, Sicily, on their lovely back patio beside palm and olive trees, steps from the sea. One memorable couscous dish they served had stewed vegetables with chopped pistachios on top. Pistchios are grown nearby, and I loved the added crunch.

CARROT-PISTACHIO COUSCOUS

Sauté

on med heat, stirring frequently, about 7 min or until carrots are a bit tender

1 red onion (thinly sliced)
5 rainbow carrots (sliced in ovals)
2 cloves garlic (minced)
olive oil
coarse salt

Cook

1 c (135 g) pearl couscous according to package instructions (which is usually simmering with 1½ c (360 ml) liquid for about 10 min). I like to use vegetable broth instead of water to add flavor.

Serve

Toss the cooked couscous with a bit of olive oil to keep it from clumping, then spread it out on a platter & pile the vegetables on top. Sprinkle the platter with ¼ c (30 g) roasted, salted pistachios that have been coarsely chopped, plus 2 T chopped parsley & lemon wedges to squeeze on top. Serve immediately, while hot.

Santa Maria La Scala, Sicily

grilled
VEGETABLE &
cheese
PLATTER

Cut the bell pepper into slabs & all else into ¼-in (6-mm) slices. Grill using a BBQ or a grill pan with olive oil, salt & pepper

2 bell peppers
1 small eggplant
2 red potatoes
1 small red onion
1 zucchini

Arrange the grilled vegetables on a platter with a 6-oz (170-g) round of soft cheese like Brie. Drizzle honey over all & sprinkle on a couple pinches of dried oregano. I like to eat this as an appetizer, using the vegetable slices in place of crackers with the cheese, but it can also be served at the table with forks and knives. Serve warm or at room temp.

At restaurants in Sicily, I often ordered a grilled vegetable plate, and usually it came with slices of potato, which I found to be a surprising and delicious addition! One such dish in Cefalù at Galleria Ristorante came drizzled with honey and dried oregano, such a simple yet flavorful seasoning.

Pan con Tomate

We had this tapa to start many meals in Spain. Pan con tomate (in Spanish) or pa amb tomàquet (in Catalan) is quite simple but does vary from place to place. The type of bread varies and may or may not be toasted, the tomato might be grated, sometimes there is garlic, and occasionally you prepare it yourself at the table. A friend who grew up in Barcelona showed me how her family makes it, which is what I am sharing here. They use a very specific type of small, juicy tomato for this recipe, and vines of them are sold on strings in the markets. This dish is only as good as the quality of the ingredients, so if you can, splurge on a nice baguette from a bakery, best-quality olive oil, and ripe, in-season tomatoes.

8 small tomatoes
Look for a smaller variety like Campari, Plum, or Roma & cut them in half.

1 baguette
cut into ½-inch (12-mm) slices

8 cloves garlic
cut in half lengthwise

cut

On a platter, set out the above ingredients plus a small bowl of salt (I use Maldon or kosher) & a small bottle of olive oil. Show guests how to prepare their own tomato bread. Start by rubbing a sliced garlic clove (cut side down) on a slice of bread. Then vigorously squeeze & rub a tomato on the bread leaving lots of seeds & juice. Next add a pinch of salt, followed by a good amount of olive oil. The garlic & tomato halves can each be used on 2 or 3 slices of bread. Optional: top each tomato bread with a thin slice of Manchego cheese.

dish at right was photographed on a Gaudi bench in Barcelona (see page 245, bottom right) ⟶

Baked Provolone

We saw vessels of melted Provolone cheese on tapas menus all over Barcelona.
It hardens relatively quickly, so enjoy it right as it comes out of the oven!

YOU'LL NEED:

2 cloves garlic, minced

8 oz (225 g) sliced Provolone

1 T chopped fresh oregano

1 T chopped fresh chives

1 baguette, sliced

Sprinkle the minced garlic between the slices of Provolone & layer them
inside a small (approx 6-in/15-cm) oiled skillet or baking dish. Sprinkle the
top with oregano, chives & black pepper. Bake at 400°F (205°C) for 10-15 min or
until bubbly & melted. Dip slices of baguette (toasted or not) in the cheese
& use a knife to cut into it as it hardens.

BURRATA BAR

At the beautiful and bustling indoor market Mercado de San Miguel in Madrid, Spain, there were booths offering nothing but burrata, served many different ways, but mostly as appetizers and often atop crostini. Burrata is perhaps my favorite cheese; it's similar to fresh mozzarella on the outside but has a creamy ricotta-like center. It can be paired with sweet or savory toppings and is great on toasted bread. In my opinion, you can never have enough of it, and I'm glad Spain thinks so, too!

burrata

olive oil + balsamic

tomatoes
apple
arugula

capers

Flaky or kosher salt

pine nuts

baked garlic head

(cut off the top, drizzle with oil & bake 45 min at 400°F/220°C)

fig jam

Pesto
(I use store-bought)

roasted red peppers
(from a jar)

OTHER IDEAS:
black pepper
peaches
figs
olives
marinara
caramelized onions
fresh thyme
sesame seeds

A burrata bar is a fun, interactive appetizer when entertaining. It's great for a small group around a coffee table. Set out the burrata cheese (budget at least 2 oz/55 g per person) plus crostini. I make the crostini by toasting baguette slices (that have been drizzled with oil and salt) on one side under the broiler. Serve several small bowls of toppings and let guests build their own appetizers. Here are a few flavor combination suggestions:

roasted red pepper, pesto & pine nuts

fig jam, arugula, salt & pepper

baked garlic & capers

apple & pine nuts

pesto, baked garlic & pepper

tomato, arugula, olive oil & balsamic

Burrata & Olive Antipasto

Two of my favorite meals in Barcelona were at Lolita Taperia in the Sant Antoni neighborhood and Tapeo in El Born. They both served delicious burrata appetizers and I have combined my favorite components of each to create this simple dish.

1. { chop 1 handful of yellow **CHERRY TOMATOES** & lay them out in the center of a small plate

2. { place a 4-oz (115-g) ball of **BURRATA CHEESE** on top of the tomatoes

3. { place a spoonful of store-bought **OLIVE TAPENADE** on top of the cheese, plus a sprinkling of chopped chives & a big drizzle of olive oil

serve with baguette slices that have been pan-fried in olive oil or toasted

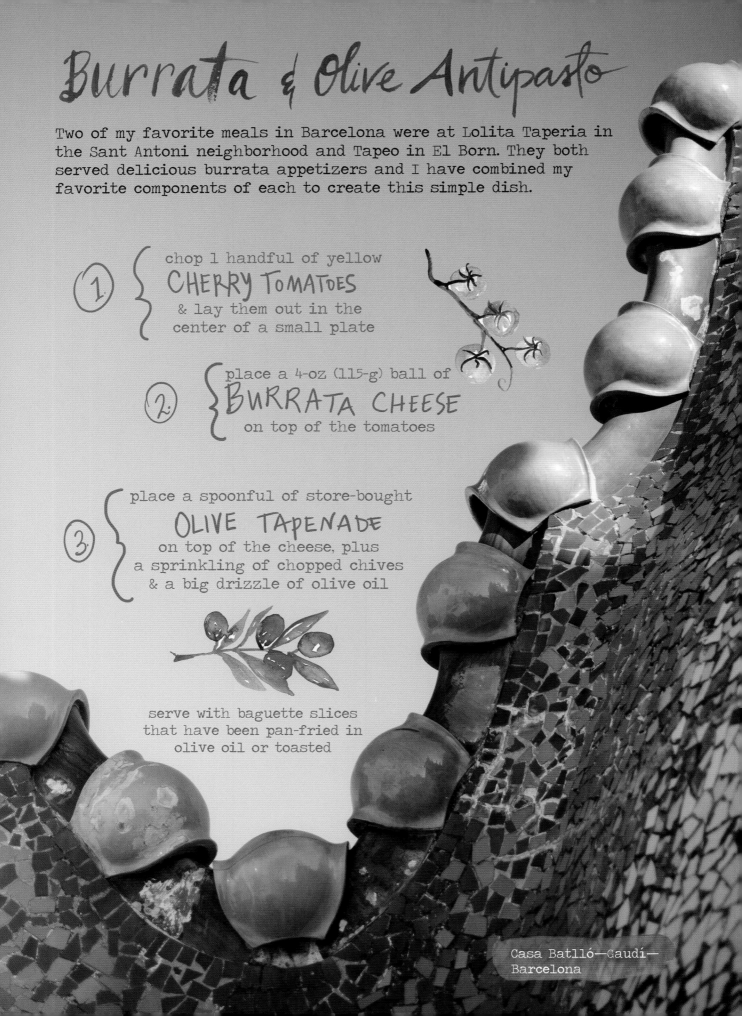

Casa Batlló—Gaudí—Barcelona

Butternut + Burrata PLATTER

① peel & cube ½
BUTTERNUT SQUASH →

(about 3 c/345 g of
1-in/2½-cm cubes)

② ROAST
the cubes
on a baking sheet
with a generous amount of
OLIVE OIL
plus a bit of salt & pepper
at 425°F (220°F) for 30-40 min
(tossing once)
or until fork-tender &
a bit browned

③ arrange the roasted squash
on a platter or cutting
board with 8 oz (225 g) of
BURRATA CHEESE
& a handful of fresh arugula

serve

with grilled, toasted, or pan-fried slices
of rustic bread, plus a fork & knife
& additional salt, pepper & olive oil so
guests can build their own toasts

We saw many variations of potato croquettes on tapas menus all over Spain. They often include small bits of ham, so this is my vegetarian adaptation. They usually have a longer shape, but I find them easier to make when rolled into small balls.

Mushroom Croquettes

1 Russet potato
1 sweet potato
} peel, cube & boil in water for about 10 min or until soft

½ red onion
6 cremini mushrooms
} dice & sauté with olive oil & salt over med heat, about 5 min

MASH the potatoes with a fork then stir in the cooked onion-mushroom mixture, plus salt & pepper. Allow to cool a bit, then roll into 1-T balls. Dip each ball first in beaten egg (you'll need about 2), then in breadcrumbs (you'll need about 1 c/100 g).

FRY the balls in a pan with a thin layer of olive oil, on med heat, turning a few times, until browned & crispy. Enjoy right away with a dipping sauce. Choose one from page 22 or simply mix Greek yogurt with hot sauce.

Ezra and me swimming in Sitges, Spain

FIG CAKE
with dried cherries

On a day trip from Barcelona, we visited the stunning mountainside monastery called Montserrat (below). We took a cable car to the top, where there were tables selling an impressive variety of little round dried fig cakes (pan de higo), each uniquely decorated with dried fruit and nuts. Thin slices of this cake are often used instead of a cracker with cheese. We brought some home to enjoy as an appetizer before dinner with wine. I added dried cherries to my variation for a bit of tang.

Dried Mission Figs
1 c (100 g), stems removed

dried cherries
¼ c (35 g), unsweetened

roasted almonds
½ c (70 g), unsalted

plus... a pinch of cinnamon, 1 T honey & 1 T water

Blend all the ingredients in a food processor until a sticky dough-like consistency is achieved. If the mixture seems too dry, add a tiny bit more water. Using your hands, form it into a big patty. Decorate the top by pressing in more dried fruit and nuts. I used whole pine nuts, almonds & a slice of dried fig. Wrap & chill before serving, which makes it harden and easier to slice. Serve with wedges of Manchego cheese.

ONION + FIG Tartines

All over the French Riviera I saw variations on the idea of an open-faced sandwich, or tartine. The size of the bread slices varied, as well as the toppings. With a glass of rosé, to me, this is a perfect light meal.

1. very thinly slice ½ large onion (use a mandoline if you have one)

2. sauté the onion for 15 min on med/low heat, stirring often, with:

   { 1 T BUTTER
   1 T OLIVE OIL
   1 T BALSAMIC

3. toast 4 slices of crusty French bread & top each slice (in this order) with: 2 T goat cheese, 1 T fig jam, a spoonful of the onions, a pinch of pine nuts, a drizzle of olive oil, plus salt & pepper to taste.

The restaurant Le Galet in Nice, France

This recipe is inspired by a mushroom toast I had at a restaurant while staying in the Algarve region of southern Portugal. Instead of a poached egg, theirs was served with a raw egg yolk on top.

Mushroom-Shallot Toast

sauté 2 min on med/low heat:

1 large diced shallot
2 T butter

then add to the pan:

3 cremini mushrooms
1 shiitake mushroom   CHOPPED
1 Portobello mushroom
1 clove garlic (minced)
2 T olive oil
1 t fresh thyme

Sauté 10 min, stirring often, or until the mushrooms are reduced in size, soft & slightly browned. Pile spoonfuls of the mushroom mixture onto 4 slices of toasted, buttered bread & top each with a fried or poached egg, salt & pepper.

Praia da Luz, Portugal

Stone Fruit BRUSCHETTA

I like the sweetness added by replacing the typical tomato in bruschetta with stone fruit. The garlic adds a delicious and somewhat unexpected kick of flavor.

1 c (155 g) diced stone fruit
(I used 3 peaches, but you could also use plums, nectarines, apricots, or a mix)

3 cloves garlic
sliced paper thin

2 T chopped basil

2 t olive oil

salt & pepper

Mix all the ingredients in a bowl, then spoon onto slices of toasted baguette that have been sprinkled with olive oil & salt.

GREENS + BEANS TARTINES

1. Fry 4 thick slices of a rustic French-style bread (like sourdough) on med heat in a pan with some olive oil & butter until golden on both sides. Remove the bread from the pan, but keep it hot.

FIRST BREAD

THEN BEANS + CHARD

2. PLACE IN THE PAN:

GARLIC — 3 cloves, minced

BEANS — ⅔ c (100 g) drained, rinsed cannellini beans from a can

CHARD — 4 large stalks, leaves & stems cut into thin ribbons

LEMON — juice from ½ lemon

(plus a sprinkle of olive oil, salt & pepper)

Sauté for about 2 min on med/low heat, until beans are warmed & greens are wilted. Pile the mixture onto the toasted bread slices & top each with a squeeze of lemon, a drizzle of oil & a pinch of salt & pepper. Enjoy warm.

145

One memorable meal on our trip was at a restaurant called Le Galet on the promenade in Nice, France (below), perhaps because of the seaside setting, but also because it was so delicious. It's actually an Italian restaurant, potentially influenced by the fact that the Italian border is so close. I had an eggplant pizza with a glass of rosé that I am still dreaming about. I was inspired to create an appetizer version once I returned to California.

eggplant pizzette

Slice 1 eggplant into ¼-in (6-mm) rounds & pan-fry 6 slices over med heat with olive oil, salt & pepper until lightly golden on both sides.

Separate 16 oz (455 g) store-bought pizza dough into 6 pieces & on a lightly floured surface roll each into a small disc just slightly larger than the eggplant rounds.

Place the dough rounds on an oiled baking sheet & top each with about 1 T marinara sauce & 1 eggplant slice. Bake at 425°F (220°C) for 15–20 min (or according to dough's package instructions). Remove from the oven & top each with a piece of burrata or fresh mozzarella cheese, olive oil & red pepper flakes (or the spicy oil on pg. 22).

Le Galet, Nice, France

BROCCOLINI
stuffed flatbread

FINELY CHOP & SAUTÉ 2-3 MIN ON MED/LOW

{
5 scallions
1 bunch broccolini (or broccoli rabe)
2 cloves garlic
olive oil
salt & pepper

Roll out 16 oz (455 g) store-bought whole-wheat PIZZA DOUGH into 2 (10-in/25-cm) rounds. Spread the broccolini mixture out on one round then sprinkle with 2 oz (55 g) crumbled FETA. Place the other dough round on top & pinch the edges. Sprinkle with grated PARMESAN, salt & pepper. Bake on an oiled sheet at 425°F (220°C) for about 15 min, until golden. Cut into wedges & serve warm. You can also serve this with marinara or pesto as a dipping sauce.

While meandering the cobbled walkways in the seaside town of Portovenere, Italy, I popped into a bakery for a quick snack and ended up sampling torta di riso for the first time. It's a type of **rice pie** common in Liguria and I saw both sweet (with cinnamon and sugar) and savory (with cheese) variations. It's a great way to use up **leftover rice** and you can be creative with additions. I added greens to mine and find it's lovely alongside a salad or a filling snack on-the-go.

Spinach - Rice Pie

4 c (800 g) cooked short-grain brown rice
½ diced onion sautéed with 1 T oil for 10 min on low
⅓ c (15 g) grated Parmesan
3 eggs, beaten
handful of baby spinach, finely chopped
½ t garlic powder
pinch nutmeg
salt & pepper

Mix all ingredients

then spread the mixture out into an oiled 9-in (23-cm) pie dish.

Bake 35-40 min at 350°F (175°C)

Tap the top with your finger to make sure it is firm, then remove from the oven. It's best warm, but also works at room temperature.

Pissaladière

Around the corner from where we stayed in Antibes, France, there was the prettiest boulangerie (bakery) that sold sheet pans full of this savory onion tart. My version has capers instead of the traditional anchovies.

makes 4 (4-in/10-cm) pieces

Slice 2 large onions using a mandoline (or very thinly with a knife) & sauté on med/low heat with 3 T oil, plus a pinch of salt & pepper, for 20 min, stirring often.

then mix in:

- 1 clove garlic, minced
- ½ t chopped fresh rosemary
- ½ t fresh thyme
- 1 T capers

Sauté with the onions for 2 more min

Prepare an 8-in (20-cm) puff pastry sheet on a greased baking sheet by pinching up the edges to form a crust. Spread the onion mixture over the dough. Decorate the top with kalamata olives & thin slices of red bell pepper arranged in Xs.

Bake at 400°F (205°C) for 20 min

I would love to go back to the cafe at the National Tile Museum in Lisbon (see page 216) for its custardy quiche and beautiful setting. These savory tartlets are inspired by that quiche and the pastels de nata (sweet mini custard pies, page 245, top right) you can find all over Lisbon. Mine are unassumingly veggie-packed, which might make my kids more apt to try them.

Squash & Custard Tartlets

makes 8-10

1.
2 eggs
¾ c (180 ml) heavy cream
1 yellow crookneck squash, finely grated & squeezed
pinch nutmeg
salt & pepper

2. I use a thin dish towel to squeeze as much liquid out of the raw squash as possible. You should end up with about ½ c (65 g) tightly packed grated squash.

Mix all ingredients

3. Using a large jar lid, cut 8-10 rounds from 1 sheet of PUFF PASTRY from a 17-oz (490-g) box. Press them inside a greased muffin tin & pour the filling into each.

4. Bake 25 min at 350°F (175°C)

or until the egg is set & the edges are slightly golden

enjoy warm

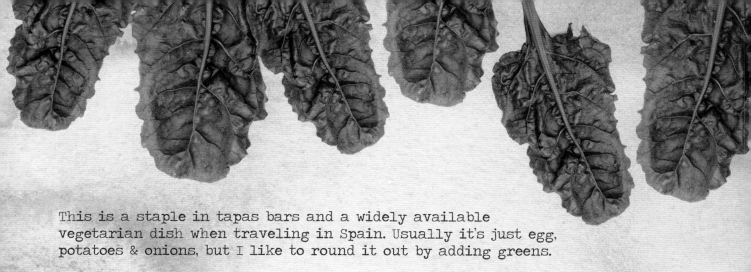

This is a staple in tapas bars and a widely available
vegetarian dish when traveling in Spain. Usually it's just egg,
potatoes & onions, but I like to round it out by adding greens.

Tortilla Española
WITH RAINBOW CHARD

Slice 3 small red potatoes
& 1 small red onion into very
thin circles (I use a mandoline).

Using a 9-in (23-cm) (preferably nonstick) skillet, fry the potatoes
& onions with salt, pepper & 3 T olive oil on low heat for about
15 min, stirring frequently. When the potatoes are fork-tender,
add 2 big rainbow chard leaves that have been very thinly sliced.
Stir & cover until wilted (about 2 min). Turn the burner off.

Next, beat 6 eggs in a mixing bowl with a bit of salt & pepper
then transfer the hot potato mixture to the bowl. Stir. Scrape
the skillet to remove any browned pieces that remain then return
to a low heat, adding 2 T olive oil to coat the pan. When hot, pour
the egg mixture into the skillet. Cover tightly with a lid & let
cook on low for 5-8 min. Using a spatula, check to see if the bottom
is browning a bit. When it seems mostly intact, using pot holders,
place a large plate on the pan & very carefully flip the pan
over, transferring the tortilla to the plate, then slide it back
into the pan to cook the other side (uncovered) for about 3 min.
Cut in wedges, salt to taste & enjoy hot!

Meat-filled empanadas are a baked tapas dish often found in northern Spain. They can easily be made vegetarian and filled with almost any type of vegetable, or even made sweet by filling with fruit & nuts.

Portobello Empanadas

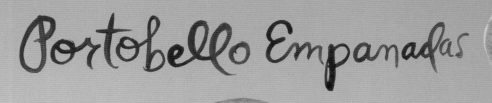

2 Portobello caps
½ onion
2 cloves garlic

1. Dice & sauté with 3 T olive oil & a pinch of salt & pepper on med/low. After 10 min, stir in ½ c (75 g) golden raisins. Then cook for another 10 min, or until the mushrooms have reduced & are soft.

2. Remove from heat & stir in ½ c (55 g) shredded sharp cheddar cheese. Allow to cool a bit.

3. Unroll 2 (9-in/23-cm) store-bought pie crusts (from a box) & cut them in quarters. Spoon the mushroom onto one half of each crust triangle, then fold over & pinch the edges. Lay them out on a baking sheet & poke each with a fork.

cut

cut

4. Bake at 375°F (190°C) for 15–20 min or until golden. Enjoy alone or with a dipping sauce like yogurt (plain or mixed with hot sauce).

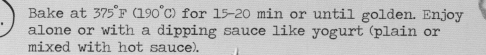

While staying on the Côte d'Azur in Antibes, France, we were steps from the farmers' market and shopped there daily. On certain days a portable oven was there, and they made fresh savory chickpea pancakes on the spot. This healthy, gluten-free street food is typical to the region and was served simply with black pepper on top. I added rosemary to mine because I saw so much of it growing around this seaside village. In Italy they have an almost identical dish called farinata, which we saw on the nearby Ligurian coast.

Rosemary Socca

1 c (90 g) chickpea flour
1 c (240 ml) warm water
2 T olive oil
1 t chopped fresh rosemary
pinch of salt

MIX
& let sit 30 min

Meanwhile...

Preheat the oven to 450°F (230°C) with a small (11-in/28-cm) cast-iron skillet inside. When the batter is ready, carefully add 2 T olive oil to coat the hot skillet then pour the batter in. Bake for 10-12 min or until fully set. Cut into wedges & serve warm, sprinkled with black pepper. It's best eaten with a topping or dip such as pesto, jam, or creamy cheese (see page 126 for ideas). It also makes a great crust for a gluten-free pizza.

Antibes, France

here & right:
socca at the
market in
Antibes, France

here: Antibes, France
left: items we brought
home from the market
in Antibes

At Le Tilleul in Saint-Paul-de-Vence, France, we had a salad with wrapped goat cheese that inspired the one on page 78.

The tiled outdoor kitchen at
the villa we stayed at in Sicily

PASTA

A highlight of my time in Italy was taking a pasta class with Chef Luca Sturlese at a cooking workshop space in Manarola called A Pié de Campu. I learned how to make a few different kinds of pasta by hand (see page 168). Using a mortar and pestle, we also made a typical Ligurian walnut sauce with marjoram (page 23).

Back in the woods at home, I invited some friends over for a pasta-making night on the deck. We drank Italian wine and made Pistachio Pesto (page 23) to go with it.

FRESH ≷EGG≷ PASTA

(just flour, eggs + salt!)

1. Put 2 c (250 g) flour & ½ t salt in a bowl. Stir, then make a well in the center & crack in 4 large eggs.

2. Using a fork, slowly whisk the eggs, pulling in the flour little by little.

3. Use your hands to form a ball (it's OK if some crumbs remain). Transfer to a lightly floured board & knead at least 8 min (I set a timer). If it seems sticky, add pinches of flour as you go. If it seems dry, wet your hands & keep kneading. It should be soft like Play-Doh & relatively easy to knead.

4. Shape the dough into a ball, cover in plastic wrap & let rest for 30 min.

5. Cut the dough ball in quarters & one at a time, on a floured surface, roll each out as thinly as possible. Sprinkle flour on both sides & fold the flat rounds in half, then continue rolling. Unfold & repeat, folding the opposite way. Do this a few times until it's quite thin. Be sure to add flour as you go so it doesn't stick together.

FOLD & CONTINUE ROLLING

* USE FLOUR

6. Next, roll each thin slab up like a jelly roll & slice very thinly. Unravel the coils & boil in salted water for 3 to 4 min. Serve with your favorite sauce or simply with olive oil, salt, pepper, Parmesan & red pepper flakes.

When in Genoa, we came to realize that the "proper" way to eat pesto Genovese is with a specific type of tightly spiraled pasta called trofie. We tried it for the first time among the locals at the restaurant Il Genovese near Piazza Colombo, where we were lucky to get a table during their busy lunch rush. My adaptation of the dish includes some additions that make it a meal.

TROFIE WITH PESTO

Boil together:

- 8 oz (225 g) trofie pasta
- 2 c (280 g) halved mini potatoes (should be about 1-in/2½-cm pieces)

Cook according to the pasta's package instructions, but for about 10 min, or until the potatoes are fork-tender & pasta is al dente

when they're done, turn the heat off & stir in 1½ c (165 g) trimmed, sliced green beans. Cover & let sit 1 min.

Strain all & toss with ¼ c (60 ml) pesto (store-bought or homemade). Serve hot.

Orzo Risotto

serves 4 as a side

1. Melt 2 T butter in a large skillet.

2. Add 1 c (180 g) dry orzo & stir to coat.

3. Add 2 c (480 ml) vegetable broth & simmer on low 10 min or until orzo is al dente & broth is evaporated. Stir occasionally & add more broth if necessary.

    With 2 min left, add 5 asparagus stalks that have been thinly sliced into "coins." Stir.

4. Remove from the heat & stir in:

    ⅓ c (30 g) grated Parmesan
    2 t olive oil
    zest from 1 lemon
    a bit of salt & pepper

serve hot

Manarola, Italy

SPAGHETTI with Lentil "MEATBALLS"

makes about 15 balls
serves 5

Countries around the Mediterranean have their own way of making and serving meatballs. In Spain, we saw albondigas on tapas menus, sometimes served in a sauce with toothpicks. In Italy, polpette may be served alone or even in soup. This is my vegetarian twist on the common dish, served with pasta.

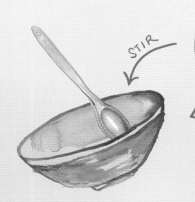

STIR

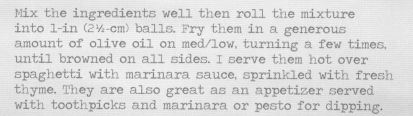

LENTILS 1⅓ c (264 g) cooked brown lentils (I used a 15-oz/425-g can, drained)

BREADCRUMBS ½ c (50 g)

EGG 1 big one!

GARLIC ½ t garlic powder or 2 minced cloves

RED PEPPER FLAKES a big pinch (or to taste)

SALT a couple pinches of kosher salt

PEPPER a few grinds

Mix the ingredients well then roll the mixture into 1-in (2½-cm) balls. Fry them in a generous amount of olive oil on med/low, turning a few times, until browned on all sides. I serve them hot over spaghetti with marinara sauce, sprinkled with fresh thyme. They are also great as an appetizer served with toothpicks and marinara or pesto for dipping.

Toledo, Spain

BEET
pasta

Boil   8 oz (225 g) pasta
(I used long fusilli)

Grate   1 small beet using a fine grater (no need to peel)

Drain   the pasta then put it back in the hot pot

Add   the grated beet, juice from ½ lemon, 2 oz (55 g) goat cheese, 2 T olive oil, plus salt & pepper to taste

Serve
topped with fresh
herbs (I used parsley)

Castelbuono, Sicily

brussels sprouts
PAPPARDELLE

① Slice

8 oz (225 g) Brussels sprouts
very thinly, until shredded.
(should come to about 2 c)

② Sauté

on med/high (stirring often)
with about 2 T olive oil, plus a pinch
of salt & pepper, for 3-5 min, until
wilted with a few crispy bits.

③ Toss

the cooked sprouts with
8 oz (225 g) cooked pappardelle
pasta (preferably fresh pasta),
a splash of olive oil, salt &
pepper. Top with shavings of
Pecorino cheese. Serve hot.

Cefalù, Sicily

gnocchi + cauliflower
CASSEROLE

1 small head cauliflower
cut into florets, about 4 c (530 g)

gnocchi

a 17-oz (480 g) package

Parmesan
1 c (100 g) grated

In a big pot of water, boil the cauliflower
for 3 min then throw in the gnocchi. Cook for
2 more min or until the gnocchi floats, then
turn the burner off & strain everything. Put
the cauliflower & gnocchi back in the hot pot &
stir in ¾ c (70 g) of the Parmesan plus 2 T butter,
2 t olive oil, several grinds of black pepper &
a couple pinches of salt. Spread the mixture
into an 8 x 8-in (20 x 20-cm) casserole dish.
Sprinkle the remaining ¼ c (30 g) Parmesan on
top plus a bit more salt & pepper. Broil for
3 min or until the top is golden.

serve hot

Cinque Terre, Italy

When visiting the hilltop town of Taormina in Sicily, we had lunch outside on the main pedestrian walkway, Corso Umberto. I ordered pasta alla Norma, a Sicilian pasta dish with eggplant. It came with a thick tomato sauce and shavings of some amazing aged ricotta salata, a hard, salty type of ricotta cheese. My version skips the sauce and includes warmed tomatoes instead, and plenty of ricotta salata.

Pasta alla Norma

1. Boil → 8 oz (225 g) rigatoni pasta according to package instructions

2. Cube → 1 eggplant into 1-in/3-cm pieces. Fry with olive oil (at least ¼ c/60 ml) & salt on med for about 10 min, tossing until tender & browned

3. Add → 1 c (180 g) halved cherry tomatoes & 1 minced clove garlic & sauté 2 more min

toss with:
¼ c (10 g) chopped basil
¼ c (20 g) shaved ricotta salata cheese
olive oil, salt & pepper

Taormina, Sicily

Fried Ricotta gnocchi

1-in (2.5-cm)

(Use flour
to keep from sticking

2 c (490 g) whole-milk ricotta
2 eggs
1 c (100 g) grated Parmesan
1 c (125 g) flour
pinch of salt

Mix in a bowl to form a dough. If it
feels too sticky to roll into a log,
add a bit more flour.

roll the dough into a log
& slice into 1-in (2½-cm) pieces

Bring a pot of salted water to a boil & cook the gnocchi in batches,
waiting until they float (about 3 min). Meanwhile, melt 2 T butter in a
pan. Drain the gnocchi, pat them dry & transfer to the pan & cook until
browned, turning a couple times. Enjoy them right away, sprinkled with
olive oil, chopped chives, salt & pepper, or your favorite sauce.

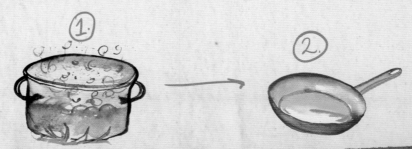

Pasta e fagioli (pasta and beans) is a common Italian combination, and we usually saw it with white beans, although you could use any kind. The beans add protein and make this a more filling dish, while the lemon zest and rind add a unique flavor boost.

serves 4 as a side

LEMONY
pasta fagioli

Very thinly slice 1 lemon into rounds (I use a mandoline & leave the peel on) & then into small triangles. Throw the triangles into a pot of boiling water & blanch for 2 min. Remove with a slotted spoon. Keep the water boiling.

Next, add 8 oz (225 g) orecchiette pasta to the water & boil according to package instructions (about 8 min).

While the pasta cooks, fry the blanched lemons in a skillet with 1 T butter & a pinch of salt until golden (about 5 min on med/low heat).

When the pasta is done, turn the heat off & add 1 (15-oz/430-g) can drained cannellini beans to the pasta water (just to warm the beans). Strain the whole pot.

mix in a bowl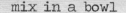

the fried lemons
hot pasta & beans
½ c (50 g) grated Parmesan
2 T olive oil
juice & zest from 1 lemon
salt & pepper

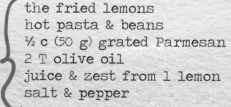

Serve right away with a bit more Parmesan, salt & pepper on top, plus chili oil (page 22), if you like it spicy. For a different twist, mix in sautéed greens, like chard, to the finished dish.

On a fun night out in Madrid, Jonathan and I stopped into a few different tapas bars in the hip and bustling neighborhood of La Latina. At one, we sat at the bar and ordered several dishes, one of which was a ramekin-sized artichoke lasagna. I hadn't seen this on menus before and thought it was such a tasty and filling snack to have with a drink.

Mini Artichoke Lasagnas

makes 4

YOU'LL NEED:

1 c (240 ml) marinara sauce
6 oz (170 g) fresh mozzarella, sliced
4 T chopped marinated artichoke hearts
4 strips of no-boil lasagna noodles, broken into pieces
½ c (50 g) grated Parmesan

Put a spoonful of marinara in the bottom of each of 4 (3½-in/9-cm) ramekins, then layer all other ingredients except the Parmesan, which goes on top. Try to give each ramekin 3 layers of noodles & always make sure some sauce is covering the noodles.

Bake at 375°F (190°c) for 25-30 min

Cool a bit before serving & top each with fresh basil, salt & pepper.

When I was studying art in Italy in college, one of my favorite pasta dishes was simply aglio, olio, e peperoncino (garlic, oil & red pepper flakes). I've started with that in mind and added some lemon and greens. You rarely see whole-wheat pasta at restaurants in Italy, but to me it feels a little lighter and is perfect for a healthy weeknight meal.

Spaghetti
with chard & garlic

Sauté

1. **Boil** 8 oz (225 g) whole-wheat spaghetti according to package instructions.

2. **Slice** 5 leaves of rainbow chard very thinly (including stalks) & sauté in olive oil on med heat with 4 cloves minced garlic for 2-3 min or until wilted. Turn off the heat.

3. **Strain** the cooked pasta & add it to the skillet with the chard. Also stir in juice from ½ lemon, 2 T grated Parmesan, a sprinkle of red pepper flakes & a bit more olive oil, salt & pepper.

Serve hot with additional lemon wedges, salt & pepper.

Gibilmanna, Sicily

On the hiking trail between the villages of Cinque Terre, Italy, we passed terraced vineyards and olive groves being harvested. For lunch we stopped in the town of Corniglia for pasta with the typical Ligurian walnut sauce at A Cantina da Mananan (bottom right & recipe on page 23).

Cinque Terre, Italy

Castelbuono, Sicily
(here & opposite)

VEGETABLE SIDES

Sicily Italy

While staying in Cefalù, Sicily, we took a drive through some small mountain towns nearby and ate at a farm near Castelbuono called Agriturismo Bergi (below). We were the only guests for lunch on that December day, and they prepared a meal just for us using ingredients from their land and wine they made themselves. We sat by a big stone fireplace as they brought out several courses, including a delicious zucchini dish with cheese and herbs that inspired this recipe. After lunch we took a walk in the citrus grove behind the farmhouse.

baked ZUCCHINI strips

① Slice

3 zucchini into slabs that are about ¼-in (6-mm) thick & 3-in (7½-cm) long

② Dip

each slab in beaten egg (you'll need about 2), then breadcrumbs mixed with grated Parmesan (about ½ c/50 g each)

③ Arrange

the slabs on an oiled baking sheet & sprinkle salt, pepper, garlic powder & more Parmesan over all. Bake at 425°F (220°C) for 15 min or until golden & crispy. Serve hot, sprinkled with fresh parsley and/or marinara sauce.

honey-lime
FRIED EGGPLANT

Cut 1 eggplant

into 1-in (2½-cm) pieces & fry on
med in a large skillet with
a generous amount of olive oil
(I use about ½ c [120 ml], adding a
little at a time as I stir). Turn
the pieces a few times until
golden & crispy on a couple
sides, about 10 min.

Transfer the eggplant pieces
to a platter then sprinkle with:

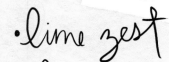

- **lime zest**   from 1 small lime
- **honey**   about 1 T
- **flaky salt**   I like Maldon brand

One of our favorite meals in Barcelona was at the restaurant Tapeo in the
historic El Born neighborhood, which came recommended by several friends.
One of the tapas I loved most there was an eggplant dish with honey and
lime, which I had to try to re-create. The flavor combination is so simple and
delicious! We saw a similar dish at another favorite restaurant, Lolita
Taperia, that used molasses instead of honey (and no lime). Both were served
as an appetizer with a toothpick, but this dish could also be served as a
side to any entreé.

PARMESAN-CRUSTED TOMATOES

with eggplant + greens

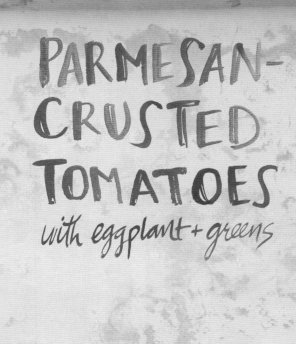

3 Roma tomatoes

3 c (175 g) baby kale

1 eggplant

FOR THE TOMATOES: Halve the tomatoes & lay them cut-side up on a baking sheet. Sprinkle with Parmesan (about 2 t on each half) & pepper. Broil until bubbly & golden, 2–3 min.

FOR THE KALE: Throw the kale in a hot pan with a bit of olive oil, a pinch of salt & a splash of water. Cover & steam, stirring a couple times, until wilted, 2–3 min.

FOR THE EGGPLANT: Remove the stem & slice it lengthwise into 6 wedges. Lay the wedges skin-side down on an oiled baking sheet & drizzle generously with olive oil, plus a couple pinches of salt & pepper. Roast at 400°F (205°C) for 25–30 min, until softened & browned.

This colorful platter of vegetables works well to accompany any entrée. Serve warm or at room temp with a small dish of romesco sauce (page 23) or marinara.

Herbes de Provence
WINTER VEGETABLES

Herbes de Provence is a dried spice mixture (available in most grocery stores) with herbs typical to the Provence region of southern France. It often includes rosemary, thyme, oregano, and lavender, & it's one of my favorite additions to roasted vegetables.

BRUSSELS SPROUTS 16 oz (455 g) halved & trimmed (about 2 cups)
BUTTERNUT SQUASH ½ squash, cut in 1-in/2½-cm cubes (about 2 c/230 g)
RED ONION 1 small onion, cut into 1-in/3-cm cubes

Spread the vegetables out on a baking sheet & sprinkle with about 1½ t herbes de Provence, plus plenty of olive oil & a sprinkle of salt & pepper.

Roast at 425°F (220°C) for 25-30 min,

Saint-Paul-de-Vence, France

Sweet Potatoes
WITH FETA DRESSING

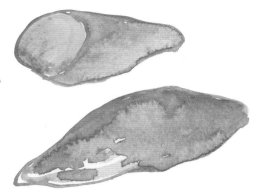

1. Cube 4 medium sweet potatoes (no need to peel) & lay out on a baking sheet. Drizzle generously with olive oil & sprinkle with salt & pepper.

2. Roast at 425°F (220°C) for 30 min or until fork-tender.

3. For the dressing, use an immersion blender to combine 2 T milk, ⅓ c (50 g) crumbled feta, 1 T olive oil, 2 t rice vinegar & a pinch of nutmeg.

   Drizzle potatoes with desired amount of dressing & sprinkle with chopped scallions.

   Serve warm or at room temp.

Lagos, Portugal

Cacio e pepe (which translates to "cheese and pepper" in Italian) is a very simple pasta dish that I have adapted to a vegetable side. Be sure to use plenty of freshly ground black pepper and a good-quality block of Parmesan cheese.

CACIO e PEPE Spaghetti Squash

Cut a med (approx 2-lb/910-g) spaghetti squash in half lengthwise & remove all the seeds & strings. Place on a baking sheet cut-side up & sprinkle with olive oil & salt.

Bake at 375°F (190°C) for 1 hour

You'll know it's done when you scrape a fork on the flesh & it separates easily into spaghetti-like "noodles." If not, cook for 10 more min. When ready, using a towel to hold the hot squash, scrape all the "noodles" into a mixing bowl.

WHILE HOT, MIX IN:
1 c (50 g) finely grated
Parmesan
2 T olive oil
1 T butter
lots of black pepper
salt

Enjoy hot

Monterosso, Sicily

SPICY *Broccolini* + LEEKS

① Slice

Thinly cut the white parts of 2 large leeks into rounds. Use a mandoline if you have one.

② Sauté

Cook the leeks on med/low with 2 T olive oil & a pinch of salt until wilted & slightly browned (about 10 min). Then add 1 bunch of broccolini (ends trimmed), plus a bit more olive oil, 2 chopped cloves garlic, a pinch of red pepper flakes, juice from ½ lemon, salt & pepper to taste. Stir & cook 3-5 min more, until the broccolini is bright green.

③ Serve

Place the broccolini on a platter with the leeks scattered on top & a small additional sprinkling of salt, pepper & red pepper flakes. Serve warm or at room temp.

2 leeks

2 cloves garlic

1 bunch broccolini

red pepper flakes

½ lemon

olive oil

CHARRED Broccoli
with onions

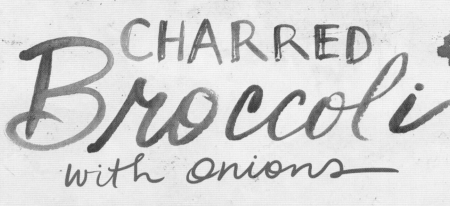

ON A BAKING SHEET:

2 heads broccoli — broken into florets

1 large red onion — sliced into medium pieces

olive oil — drizzle generously over all (at least 2 T)

red pepper flakes — sprinkle a couple pinches (about ¼ t)

garlic — sprinkle 2 minced cloves

salt & pepper — sprinkle a few pinches, to taste

BAKE AT 425°F (220°C) FOR 25 MIN, tossing once, until some edges are blackened & crispy. Enjoy right away as the florets lose crispiness as they cool.

When driving to Mount Etna in Sicily, we passed vineyards, citrus groves, ancient stone farmhouses, and rural Sicilian farmland known for its honey production, an ingredient we saw used in both sweet and savory dishes in the area. After taking in the breathtaking vista from the volcano's snowy peak, we took the 1-hour drive back down to the ocean and ended the day with a sunset walk along the water in the small town of Santa Maria La Scala.

Honey-Balsamic GREEN BEANS

green beans — 4 c (440 g) trimmed & diagonally sliced

garlic — 2 cloves, minced

① Sauté on med heat with 1 T olive oil, plus salt & pepper for 3-5 min or until the beans are bright green. Then add 1 T balsamic vinegar & 1 T honey to the pan & toss until all the beans are glazed (about 1 min).

② Transfer to a platter & sprinkle with a bit of sea salt plus:

Pomegranate — ¼ c (35 g) seeds

Pistachio — ¼ c (30 g) chopped, roasted

Santa Maria La Scala, Sicily

We were in Barcelona for the holiday of Todos los Santos (All Saints' Day), and some friends who live there invited us to their home for a traditional celebration that included baked sweet potatoes, roasted chestnuts, and pine nut cookies (panellets). Around this time, down the street from our apartment, there was a woman with a stand on the corner roasting sweet potatoes and chestnuts over hot coals. I loved how the potatoes became so dense, sweet, and blackened after being cooked for such a long time. I have subbed hazelnuts here, which are more readily available and, in my opinion, tastier.

Baked Sweet Potatoes
WITH HAZELNUTS

serves 6

①

Wash 3 medium sweet potatoes & prick them several times all over with a knife & place them on a baking sheet.

BAKE at 375°F (190°C) for 45–60 min

When a knife goes in easily, they are done.

② Slice them in half lengthwise then score them in a grid

score with a knife

③ Top each with a dollop of butter, honey, a sprinkle of cinnamon & chopped hazelnuts

here & left: Sweet potatoes & chestnuts for sale on the street in Barcelona, Spain

here: Lisbon, Portugal
left: lunch at the
National Tile Museum
in Lisbon, Portugal

Taormina, Sicily

clockwise from top left: gelato in Italy; National Palace of Pena, Sintra, Portugal; Taormina, Sicily; Cefalù, Sicily

Cefalù, Sicily

Persimmons for dessert
at Agriturismo Bergi.
Castelbuono, Sicily

SWEETS

ripe persimmon tree in Saint-Paul-de-Vence, France

avocado-
CHOCOLATE
mousse

We saw a lot of chocolate mousse in southern Portugal, which inspired me to include one in this book. This type of vegan mousse has been very popular in recent years, and this is my take on it.

AVOCADOS
flesh from 3 very ripe ones

COCOA POWDER
½ c (50 g), unsweetened

MAPLE SYRUP
¾ c (180 ml)
(or agave)

Blend in a food processor until very creamy.

Chill 1 hour before serving. Serve in small cups sprinkled with flaky Maldon sea salt & a dollop of (nondairy) whipped cream.

FROZEN *Banana* MOUSSE

it's just banana!

We went to a restaurant in southern Portugal that served several types of mousse for dessert, one of which was banana. This icy version is a popular American dessert lately that reminds me of the mousse we tasted there. It couldn't be simpler! Plus you can be creative with additions or add nothing at all and it's still delicious.

1. Peel & cut 4 ripe bananas into pieces & freeze.

2. Pulse the frozen banana pieces in a food processor, stopping & stirring several times, then blending, until very creamy.

3. Serve immediately before it starts to melt.

Optional ideas
for ingredients to pulse,
stir in, or sprinkle on top:

cinnamon
chocolate chips
coconut flakes
hazelnuts

Salema, Portugal

Honey-Pistachio Bars

makes about 16 squares

In Sicily, we drove through the Zafferana Etnea area (below), which is known for both its pistachio and honey production. We took a gondola ride to the freezing peak of the active volcano Mount Etna, which has one of the most unusual and spectacular landscape vistas I'd ever seen. Volcanic rock peeked through snow, and the sparkling sea was in the distance all around. The lodge at the top offered a tasting table with several types of local honey. My favorite was the pistachio-flavored one, which inspired this shortbread dessert.

Pulse ¾ c (95 g) roasted, salted, shelled pistachios in a food processor, then remove ¼ c (30 g) of it & set aside.

Add ½ c (100 g) sugar, 3 T honey, 2 c (250 g) flour & 1 c (2 sticks/225 g) cold butter cut into chunks to the food processor. Pulse again until well combined.

Press the crumbly mixture into an 8 x 8-in (20 x 20-cm) baking dish. Use a small cup as a rolling pin to flatten the top.

Bake at 350°F (175°C) for 30 min. Remove from the oven, sprinkle the top with the remaining pistachios and a pinch of salt, then drizzle with a bit of honey. Allow to cool 10 min, then cut into 2-in (5-cm) squares.

Mount Etna, Sicily

I first fell in love with the chocolate-hazelnut flavor combination while studying art in Italy for a year in college. I ate a lot of gianduia gelato that year! I also discovered Nutella then and now whenever I taste it, I am immediately transported back. I usually only bake if the recipe is very simple, so this dessert fits the bill with only 5 ingredients.

chocolate-hazelnut CAKE CUPS

mix in a bowl:

1 c (240 ml) Nutella

½ c (65 g) flour

2 eggs

Spoon the batter into 4 oiled (3½-in/9-cm) ramekins & bake for 18 min at 350°F (175°C). They should be just a bit molten in the middle. Allow them to cool for a minute then top each with a dollop of Nutella, a sprinkling of chopped hazelnuts & a pinch of flaky Maldon or kosher sea salt.

* enjoy warm *

Taormina, Sicily

LEMON SORBET *mimosa*

serves 1

1.

Put a couple small spoonfuls or scoops (I use a melon baller) of lemon sorbet into a champagne flute, then top with sparkling rosé.

2.

Garnish with a sprig of mint & a lemon twist then serve right away before it melts.

To make the lemon twist, carefully remove the peel from a round slice of lemon with your hands. Wrap the lemon peel around a clean pencil to form the spiral, then pull the whole thing down the pencil to remove.

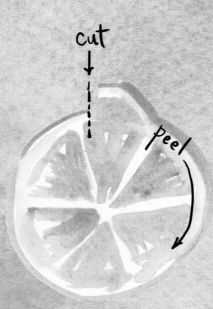

cut

Peel

Wrap

remove

When in Italy, one of my favorite ways to end a meal is with affogato, a shot of espresso poured over a scoop of gelato. Be sure to enjoy it right away, before the gelato melts completely. It's perhaps very American to ask for decaf, and I doubt an Italian would ever add banana, but for me, this is a delicious adaptation.

1. AFFOGATO split

serves 1

place a few slices of banana
in the bottom of a glass

2.

next add 2 scoops of
chocolate gelato or ice cream

3.

top with ¼ c (60 ml)
hot espresso or strong
coffee (decaf or regular)

Genoa, Italy

Monterosso al Mare, Italy

Lisbon, Portugal

Mediterranean DINNER PARTY

Once we were back home in the woods, I was eager to make some of my favorite dishes from our trip and invite friends over.

menu

Aperol Spritzes, page 50
Pan con Tomate with Manchego, page 124
Spicy Melon Salad, page 100
Shaved Snap Pea Salad, page 88
Gnocchi & Cauliflower Casserole, page 180
Avocado-Chocolate Mousse, page 222

We made Aperol Spritzes with a more traditional garnish of an orange twist & a green olive.

Decorate the buffet table and the dining table with a grouping of lemons and fresh herbs. I used lavender, flowering dill & rosemary, plus a few votives.

DIY Pan con Tomate board

We made a separate buffet table to keep things casual and easy. Everything can be served at room temperature, except keep the casserole warm in the oven until it's time to eat.

TRAVEL GUIDE

Some favorite spots in the countries we visited during the fall of 2017
See our itinerary on page 15

SPAIN

While in Spain, we visited Barcelona and Madrid. In Barcelona we loved staying in the Eixample neighborhood, a bit outside the busy downtown area, near the border of El Poble-sec. From Barcelona we did side trips to Girona, Sitges, and the Costa Brava. In Madrid we stayed in the Salamanca neighborhood and did a day trip by train to Toledo.

BARCELONA:
Our favorite meals were at Lolita Taperia, Picnic, Café Flanders (to sit outside), Tapeo (for nice tapas), La Tasqueta de Blai (for pintxos; see page 30), Tarannà Café, and Bar Calders. For drinks, try Xixbar (for gin cocktails) and Lambicus (for beer). Many evenings we sat outside near our apartment for a drink and patatas bravas at Malasaña (they have a playground out front).

Our favorite stops to see Gaudi's work were Park Güell (pages 34, 71) and Casa Batlló (page 130). We loved wandering around the huge Montjuïc park where you can visit the museum Fundació Joan Miró, take a cable car ride, visit MNAC, and see the magic fountain display after dark at Font Màgica de Montjuic. On a warm day we enjoyed sitting on the beach in the Barceloneta neighborhood, and one evening we went to a soccer match at the Camp Nou stadium (an exciting cultural experience!).

From Barcelona we did day trips by train to the Montserrat Monastery (page 136), Girona (page 14; have lunch at Federal Café) and Sitges (adorable beach town; page 134). We rented a car for an overnight trip to the Costa Brava area where we stayed in the beautiful medieval village of Besalú, drove between the seaside towns, and stopped for a sunset drink on the water in Calella de Palafrugell. I could have spent much longer on the Costa Brava and would love to go back.

MADRID:
Eat at Ana la Santa, La Cocina de San Antón (atop the San Antón market), and La Galería in El Retiro Park and have a drink on the roof terrace at Círculo de Bellas Artes. We spent one fun evening tapas-bar hopping in the La Latina neighborhood, near Calle Cava Baja. Of all the markets, Mercado de San Miguel was my favorite, and a great stop for drinks and small bites (page 128). I loved the indoor plants at the Atocha train station in Madrid.

FRANCE

When in France, we stayed in Antibes and did day trips to Nice, Cannes, Èze, Boit, and Saint-Paul-de-Vence.

ANTIBES:
I loved the Picasso Museum. Have cocktails and tartines at Pablo, a drink outside at Café Clemenceau, and look for the socca oven at the outdoor market (page 162).

NICE:
We loved our meal on the beach at Le Galet. When at the Matisse museum, check out the antique carousel in the adjacent olive grove.

SAINT-PAUL-DE-VENCE:
Have lunch outside at Le Tilleul (page 163) and visit the Maeght Foundation museum and sculpture garden.

ÈZE:
Visit the Jardin Exotique, a beautiful cactus garden overlooking the sea.
Eat and buy olive oil at Deli.

ITALY

While in Italy, we visited Liguria (Genoa and Cinque Terre) and Sicily. In Cinque Terre we stayed in Monterosso al Mare and took the train to the other nearby towns. In Sicily we flew into Catania and out of Palermo and did a road trip in between, with favorite stops in Santa Maria La Scala (page 212), Castelbuono (page 176), Zafferana Etnea, Taormina (page 182), Cefalù (page 219,) and the small seaside town of Mondello.

GENOA:
Eat at Il Genovese (have the trofie al pesto) then, on the same block, pick up a pastry for dessert at Pasticceria Tagliafico. Also, our kids loved the aquarium in Genoa.

CINQUE TERRE:
Eat at Ristorante Ciak (have the homemade gnocchi) and atop the tower at Torre Aurora in Monterosso al Mare. In Manarola, don't miss a sunset spritz or meal at Nessun Dorma. We highly recommend the pasta making class with chef Luca at A Piè de Campu. We also did a fantastic wine tour hike via an Airbnb experience called "Climb the Stairway to Wine Heaven" (led by Erica and Doug of Voyager Trips Cinque Terre) through the vineyards above Manarola (Page 49). I'd recommend taking the ferry to the idyllic town just south of Cinque Terre called Portovenere.

CEFALÙ:
Eat at Galleria Ristorante and get a seaside table at Il Covo del Pirata.

CASTELBUONO:
Eat at Agriturismo Bergi and visit the castle itself.

ETNA:
Be sure to take the gondola up Mount Etna, it's quite stunning. When driving there, stop for a honey tasting at Oro d'Etna in Zafferana Etnea.

TAORMINA:
We loved getting gelato and strolling the Corso Umberto before visiting Teatro Greco, the ancient Greek theater of Taormina.

PORTUGAL

We stayed in Lisbon, did a day trip by train to Sintra, and then rented a car and drove to the Algarve region in the south where we stayed in both Lagos and Praia da Luz and did day trips to several nearby towns.

LISBON:
Perhaps my favorite meal in Lisbon was lunch on the river at Topo Belém at the Belém Cultural Center, which has a modern feel. Alternatively, I loved the traditional ambience at Restaurante Bota Alta. If you don't have time to wait in line for the traditional custard pastries at Pastéis de Belém, try Manteigaria instead. We enjoyed walking around the LXFactory, an outdoor area with great shops and restaurants (eat at A Praça). I loved visiting the shop A Vida Portuguesa, as well as Livraria Bertrand (Chiado location), the oldest bookstore in the world. Be sure to visit the National Tile Museum and eat at their beautiful cafe.

SINTRA:
We could have spent more than a day here as there is so much to see, but the highlights were walking the walls of the Moorish Castle (page 24) and seeing the copper-filled kitchen at the National Palace of Pena.

THE ALGARVE:
We loved exploring different towns each day by car, including Sagres, Salema, Tavira, Aljezur, Lagos, and Praia da Luz. Eat at Casa Chico Zé in Faro (it's a unique location with a small farm out back) and Restaurante O Camilo, on a cliff above the ocean in Lagos. Be sure to do a boat tour of the grottoes out of Lagos as well—there are several small operators that offer them near the harbor. One of my favorite experiences in the Algarve was an olive oil tasting at Monterosa Olive Oil Farm in Moncarapacho (page 114).

Visit www.theforestfeast.com/travel for more tips and links and see more photos @theforestfeast #forestfeastmediterranean.

Sicily, Italy

ACKNOWLEDGMENTS

First, thank you to my husband, Jonathan, for thinking three months on the road with a baby and a toddler was no big deal! Your sense of adventure, constant support, and expert travel skills made this trip fun and easier for all of us. Thank you for booking all our flights, researching each destination, navigating our days, stopping every time I wanted to take a photo, always pushing the double stroller, and bouncing the baby to sleep so I could enjoy my rosé on the beach. I want to go everywhere with you!

Thank you to my kind and talented editor, Laura. Thank you for celebrating my tendency toward color overload and then helping me rein it in. Your ideas and guidance make my work infinitely stronger and I am so lucky to be able to collaborate with you.

Thank you to everyone at Abrams for being excited about this project when I pitched it, and for helping me bring it to life. Thank you, John Gall, Deb Wood, Connor Leonard, Denise LaCongo, Jordan Jacobson, and Mamie VanLangen. Thank you to Liam Flanagan for so expertly laying the book out and applying final touches.

Thank you so much to Alison, my amazing literary agent. Choosing to work with you is one of the best decisions I've ever made!

Thank you to all the friends and family who met us at different points along our journey in Europe. It was so much fun to travel with you: Wendy, Jim, Maddy, Arielle, Ethan, Caleb, Nicole, Mom, Dad, Ry, Andy, Meckenzie, and Ellie.

Thank you to my dear friend Jodie, who helped me so much with the cover shoot. Grazie!

Thank you to Kayoko and Yoko at Umami Mart for providing mixology consultation and the beautiful cocktail glasses on pages 51, 53, 61. Thank you to potter Sheba Solomon, for lending me so many beautiful pieces from your collection (pages 81, 87, 107, 135, 189, 191, 199, 223), and to Cara Janelle, the Barcelona potter whose plates I loved shooting my food on (see pages 37, 125, 197).

Thank you to Ricky and Mónica at Delicious & Sons for welcoming us into your home and teaching us about Spanish cooking.

Thank you to my faithful team of friends and family who recipe tested for me in their kitchens all over the world, this time from California to Tanzania! Thank you so much to Negar Katirai, Robert and Jenna Wachtel Pronovost, Margaret Jacobs, Anya and Ted Glenn, Dana Hartman, Jodie Porges, Martha Bixby, Laura Keller, Stacy Mason, Eliza Cohen, Amee Shah, Wendy Bloch, Jim Prosnit, Ted De Barbieri, Lauren Michele, Arielle Traub, Kate and Brandon Taylor, Bridget Schum, Kathleen Taylor, Tara Fogel, Dana Solomon, Dara Silverstein, Erin and Michael Wakshlag, Mary Hewlett, Jenna Weinberg, Micaela Hellman-Tincher, Maryguilia Capobianco, Shannon Gleeson, Jenna Sanders, Maddy Bloch, and Team Yang.

This book would not be possible without the love and support from my parents and my brother Ry. Thank you to the caregivers back home who so lovingly took care of our kids while I created these pages.

Thank you to my readers who followed along on this trip and my ongoing Forest Feast journey. Thank you for your sweet support and for making and sharing my recipes. Because of you, I am able to continue making cookbooks, and I am so grateful.

Cinque Terre, Italy

INDEX

Cinque Terre, Italy
right: the Algarve, Portugal

Vernazza, Italy

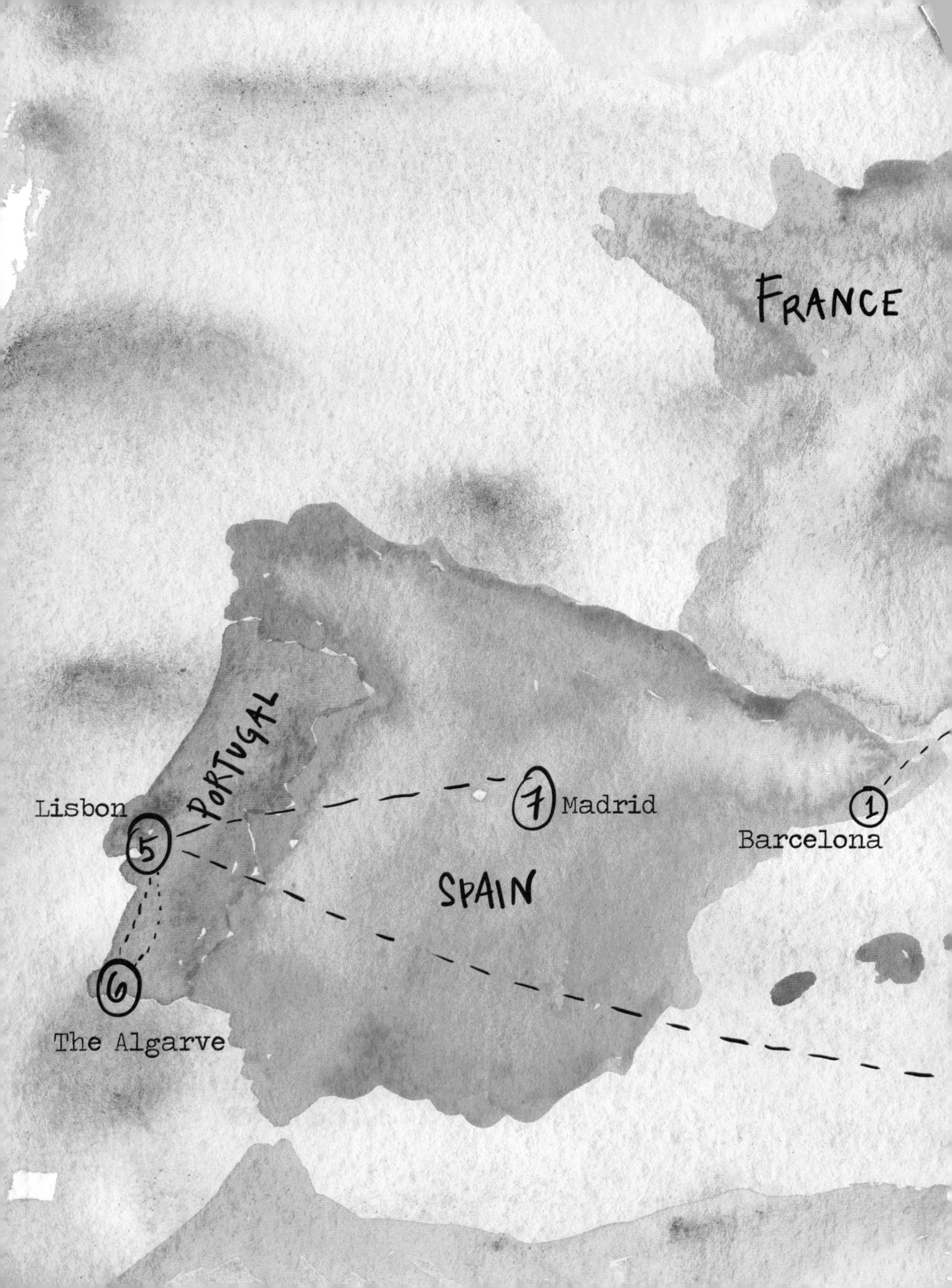
FRANCE
PORTUGAL
Lisbon
5
7
Madrid
1
Barcelona
SPAIN
6
The Algarve